ADAPTIVE
HR

First published in 2021.

ISBN: 978-1-86922-883-5 (Printed)
eISBN: 978-1-86922-884-2 (PDF ebook)

Published by KR Publishing
P O Box 3954
Randburg
2125
Republic of South Africa

Tel: (011) 706-6009
Fax: (011) 706-1127
E-mail: orders@knowres.co.za
Website: www.kr.co.za

Typesetting, layout and design: Cia Joubert, cia@knowres.co.za
Cover design: Marlene De Lorme, marlene@knowres.co.za
Editing and Proofreading: Jennifer Renton, jenniferrenton@live.co.za
Project management: Cia Joubert, cia@knowres.co.za

ADAPTIVE HR

Impactful HR for the New and Virtual World of Work

Marianne Roux

kr
publishing

2021

TABLE OF CONTENTS

ABOUT THE AUTHOR

Marianne Roux

Marianne has over 25 years global experience as a New World of Work Strategist, Leadership Educator, Transformation Consulting Director and HR Executive. She currently runs Roux Consulting, a global consulting firm with 15 collaborators around the world. She is also an Associate of Melbourne Business School, Stellenbosch Business School and Swinburne University of Technology.

Marianne has experience across several industries including Retail, FMCG, Mining, Oil and Gas, Utilities, Infrastructure, Media, Financial services, Telecommunications, Sport, NFP organisations and Tech start-ups. She has worked for PWC, Accenture, Deloitte and Mercer, and has held two HR Director roles.

She has a keen interest in the new world of work and how organisations, leaders, teams and individuals can prepare themselves for it. Her PhD research focuses on a meta model of leadership and leadership development in the new world of work.

Marianne also works pro-bono on developing women and alleviating poverty and trauma. She serves on the Board of Hagar Australia and is the founder of the Coalition of Female Social Entrepreneurs.

Marianne was chosen as one of 52 Inspirational Women at Work in South Africa in 2004, one of 20 Female Entrepreneurs by *Management Today* in 2011 in Australia, and in 2015 she won the Excellence in NFP Consulting award from the worldwide *Who's Who*.

FOREWORD

For a long time now, I have read and watched in despair how the Human Resource function is struggling to transform into a future-fit, impactful function that drives organisational agility and capability; one that helps leaders make sense of the new world of work and helps them become more human and future focused. And of course, just as I was writing this book and focusing on how Industry 4.0 is disrupting everything, the virtual age crept up on us with the COVID-19 crisis and social justice movements. This has both helped HR shine AND put us under even more pressure to respond and transform.

More than ever, an Adaptive Human Resource function can help organisations and their leaders to create value through people, as well as help create a resilient, capable and adaptive workforce that can meet any future strategies and challenges the organisation faces. With the clever use of automation and digitisation, Human Resources can improve employee service AND become a critical ally in transformation by focusing on strategic people initiatives and developing future fit leaders and teams. They can focus on co-designing compelling employee experiences, modernising critical talent processes, leveraging data and analytics, and redesigning how work gets delivered.

This is not an easy task – it will take ongoing upskilling and reskilling of all in the function and a significant change in mindset. It starts with a deep understanding of the new world of work and virtual context, the design of a competitive People Strategy for the organisation, and an HR transformation journey for the function. I found that many Human Resource professionals are not curious and informed enough about the new world of work and have spent next to no time on their own development. It is time.

For this reason, I set out to develop a course which I have been delivering around the world for the last three years called 'Adaptive HR'. This tackles the key issues I feel need attention and provides case studies and tools for Human Resource professionals to help them transform and reskill themselves, their functions and their organisations. The work has been incredible, and participants have been able to make significant shifts in their focus, work, confidence and ability. One organisation used the course to restructure their entire function and reset their People Strategy over a 12-month period. Others have used it to build new teams from scratch that contain data scientists and employee experience experts. Almost all the organisations changed the role of the business partner into a far more strategic one, and updated their HR technology to reduce administration. Many took down the barriers and silos in their function and created a fluid pool of resources that can work on changing priorities.

The time has come to spread the learnings broader and faster so that we can create a real movement of future fit HR professionals. A summary of the ideas in this book is shown in Figure 1 below. This will form our journey map through the book.

INTRODUCTION

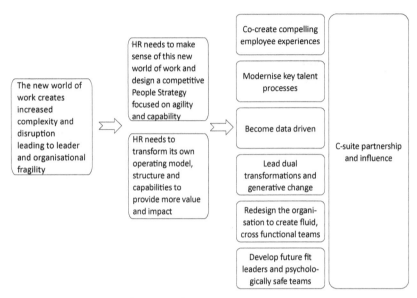

Figure 1: Becoming an adaptive HR function

In Chapter 1, I address what the new world of work and the virtual age means for organisations, employees and Human Resources. This includes an overview of the future of work, unexpected disruptions, and the need for adaptive and virtual organisations.

In Chapter 2, I address the need for strong People Strategies that drive organisational sustainability and key people imperatives that drive agility and capability. I focus in particular on the need for a wholesale redesign of work and skills in all industries and jobs.

In Chapter 3, I describe how to futureproof the Human Resource Operating Model, Structure and Capabilities in order to become a critical ally to senior leaders. I challenge the use of outdated models and urge you to reskill, upskill and transform.

In Chapter 4, I explain how to co-develop differentiated and compelling employee experiences using design thinking, employee journey mapping, personas, empathy mapping and analytics. I explain the new concept of DEX

– digital employee experiences – to give the employees a consumer grade experience.

In Chapter 5, I address the changes in talent management in the new world of work and the processes that most frustrate managers – talent acquisition and onboarding, performance management, and learning and development. I also highlight the increased importance of employee well-being and diversity, equity and inclusion as integral parts of the talent management process.

In Chapter 6, I describe the need to be a data- and analytics-driven HR function. I believe this to be a true game changer for the function – releasing Human Resource professionals from administration to deal with organisation transformation and reskilling.

In Chapter 7, I describe the work of Human Resources in leading dual transformations and generative change to renew cultures and move the organisation and employees from fragile to agile (and even anti-fragile). I also describe the use of dialogic organisational development methods as a way of changing the organisational narrative.

In Chapter 8, I tackle the difficult process of organisation design to challenge current ways of structuring organisations and the need to move to fluid, adaptive, cross-functional teams as the organising principle. This is one of the most complex processes Human Resources need to work with and well worth our while updating our approach to be future fit.

In Chapter 9, I highlight the need for an updated approach to leadership, leadership development and high performing and virtual teams in order to successfully deliver the key strategic outcomes and become fast and flexible with high levels of psychological safety and engagement.

Finally, in Chapter 10, I talk about where to start the journey and how to get the ear and support of the Board and the C-suite in order to drive the successful transformation of HR and of the organisation in the process.

I hope you enjoy this journey with me.

CHAPTER 1

The future of work and the need for Adaptive HR

The new world of work and the virtual age means significant change for organisations, employees and human resource functions. This chapter includes an overview of the future of work, unexpected disruptions and the need for adaptive, virtual and purposeful organisations. It describes the need for upskilling and reskilling employees and how HR can partner in the transformation.

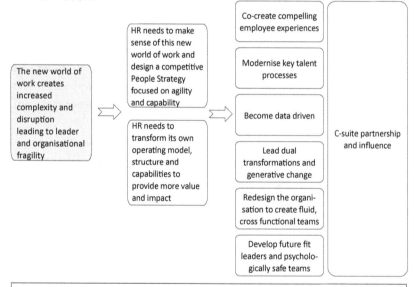

Key ideas

- The future of work and unexpected disruptions has hit harder and faster than expected and COVID-19 has heralded the start of the Virtual Age.
- There is an accelerated need to create adaptive and virtual organisations.
- Purpose as the key attractor.
- Employees will need to reskill and upskill continuously.
- HR needs to accelerate its transformation.

"The future of work is on our doorstep. With the arrival of the coronavirus crisis and enterprises' focus on business continuity, long-anticipated shifts in the world of work have, overnight, become the key to business survival. Digitalisation, remote working, and agile workforces are now essential to organizations' capacity to operate in an age of fluctuating lockdowns and economic uncertainty. As *The Economist* noted, while the CFO was the corporate hero of the 2008 financial crisis, in 2020 company leaders are looking to CHROs to secure their business in a COVID-19 impacted world."[1]

"The start of the decade has seen a convergence of three major trends: the accelerated use of Fourth Industrial Revolution technologies in the midst of the pandemic, job market disruptions to both remote work and work requiring physical presence, and a wide-ranging call for greater inclusivity, equity and social justice."[2]

"COVID-19, an event that has accelerated several aspects of the of future of health, has become the catalyst to a future of work that might otherwise have taken years to attain. Rather than a new normal, we expect the new abnormal will continue to evolve. The end-state is neither clear nor predictable."[3]

The future of work has hit harder and faster than expected and COVID-19 has heralded the start of the Virtual Age

We were in the Fourth Industrial Revolution (4IR) right up until the COVID-19 disruption. What distinguished the Fourth Industrial Revolution? Three fundamental forces characterised the transformation that was underway: the exponential nature of digital technologies meant we were experiencing change at an accelerating pace; the digital hyper-connectivity of all things and people, especially through the Internet of Things, meant increasing interdependency; and we were seeing vast digital ecosystems emerge that are still constantly evolving.[4]

---

1   Mercer, 2020.
2   World Economic Forum (WEF), 2020.
3   Mehendale & Radin, 2020.
4   Swinburne, 2019.

COVID-19 and societal pressure are accelerating this. Mehendale and Radin[5] already spoke about the virtual age – Industry 5.0, and we have not even dealt with 4.0 yet. The impact of the virtual age is that effective and strong corporate cultures need to be built that express the values of firms and there will be a need to continuously promote connectivity and interventions that can prevent isolation among employees. Some of today's work-from-home models could gravitate toward a work-from-anywhere-on-the-planet model. How we recruit and identify talent will likely go through some enormous changes, for example some organisations will adopt hybrid models where remote working is complemented by regularly bringing people together in central locations to augment the remote structure.[6]

One of the major learnings for many Execs and CEOs during the COVID-19 crisis has been that remote working 'does actually work' and this will now become the new norm in the way we work moving forward. It will also cause a reset amongst CEOs who will re-examine if they need so much office space, creating a new problem for their real estate leaders in terms of reducing the physical commercial property footprint.[7] The idea of a 9-to-5, five-day week is disintegrating and there is a significant broadening of the talent continuum and team-based structures. Branson et al. noted that: "The days of standard vacancies and permanent roles are numbered. As companies look to become more agile, and technology becomes more advanced, the concept of a job for life has gone. Instead we are increasingly seeing fluid solutions like 'Tours of Duty', and freelancers and 'gig' workers plugging in and out of organisations. What's more, crowdsourcing and open innovation are broadening the concept of work even further. This fluidity is a trend being embraced by new generations entering the workforce."[8]

There is an accelerated need for adaptive/ agile and virtual organisations

"Now we have this inherited organisational work structure that no longer aligns with the way people live and think. Companies have been moving away from this model to turn into open firms and communities, outsourcing

---

5   Mehendale & Radin, 2020.
6   Mehendale & Radin, 2020.
7   Bashinsky, 2020.
8   Branson et al., 2020.

and off-shoring their activities and implementing more flat and collaborative work organisation."[9]

"The Fifth Industrial Revolution has us all re-imagining work, workforces, and workplaces."[10]

The future of work and continuous, unexpected disruptions are accelerating the need for organisations to become adaptive/agile and virtual. Sharifi and Zhang[11] found four different generic capabilities of enterprise agility: responsiveness, competency, flexibility, and speed. Reeves and Deimler[12]

described these four organisational capabilities, which will be needed for organisations to foster rapid adaptation:

1. The ability to read and act on signals.

2. The ability to experiment rapidly and frequently – not only with products and services, but also with business models, processes and strategies.

3. The ability to manage complex and interconnected systems of multiple stakeholders.

4. The ability to motivate employees and partners.

The adaptive/agile organisation (as shown in Figure 1.1) will be the dominant organisational paradigm in the new world of work. These organisations are very different from the way we work now: roles are more fluidly defined, the overall strategy may be defined but the tactics for achieving it remain loose and flexible, decisions are made more quickly because employees are more empowered, the culture is less about judging people and more about encouraging them to be curious, and new customer needs and requirements are more likely to be anticipated. These organisations are less afraid to take risks because failing is acceptable; people and teams bounce back faster from setbacks and multiple solution options can be developed to resolve any problems.

---

9   WEC Future of Work Report, 2016.
10   Mehendale & Radin, 2020.
11   Sharifi & Zhang, 2000.
12   Reeves & Deimler, 2011.

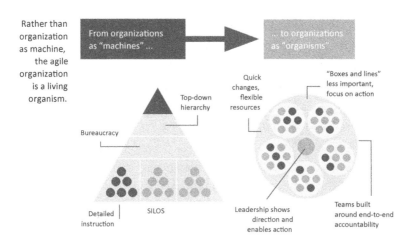

Rather than organization as machine, the agile organization is a living organism.

From organizations as "machines" ...

... to organizations as "organisms"

Top-down hierarchy

Quick changes, flexible resources

"Boxes and lines" less important, focus on action

Bureaucracy

Detailed instruction

SILOS

Leadership shows direction and enables action

Teams built around end-to-end accountability

Figure 1.1: The agile organisation is becoming the new dominant paradigm[13]

Adaptive/agile organisations mobilise quickly, are nimble and are empowered to act; they work well in the virtual age. Instead of pushing resources and people based on forecasted demand, nimble organisations may instead fluidly enable a broad range of resources and people to be pulled on an as-needed basis to respond to events in real-time and where they will have the most impact. When a problem, need or change arises, agile organisations will enable their employees to attract relevant talent to where it's needed, even if they previously weren't aware that such resources existed. Virtual and distributed work is a new reality for all and there will be a continued demand for work autonomy and flexibility, which will be further complicated by an explosion of contingent work.

Hagel et al.[14] wrote that, "To take effective advantage of technology, organisations will need to redesign work itself, moving beyond process optimization to find ways to enhance machine-human collaboration, drawing out the best of both and expanding access to distributed talent. Organizations will need to cultivate new leadership and management approaches that can help build powerful learning cultures and motivate workers to go beyond their comfort zone. Indeed, leadership styles must shift from more authoritarian – appropriate for stable work environments shaped by routine, well-defined tasks and goals – to collaborative.

---

13   Aghina, De Smet & Weerda, 2015.
14   Hagel et al., 2017, p. 40.

Heerwagen[15] summed up the key organisational changes:

- Blurred boundaries: as organisations become more laterally structured, boundaries begin to break down as different parts of the organisation need to work more effectively together. Boundaries between departments as well as between job categories (manager, professional, technical) become looser and there is a greater need for task and knowledge sharing.

- Reduced hierarchical structure: hierarchies are cumbersome and cannot respond quickly to changing market demands, such as pressures for reduced cycle time and continuous innovation. Hierarchies are being replaced by cross unit organisational groupings with fewer layers and more decentralised decision making.

- Teams as basic building blocks: the move toward a team-based organisational structure results from pressures to make rapid decisions, to reduce inefficiencies, and to continually improve work processes.

- New management perspective: workers are no longer managed to comply with rules and orders, but rather to be committed to organisational goals and missions. The blurring of boundaries also affects organisational roles. As employees gain more decision authority and latitude, managers become more social supporters and coaches rather than commanders.

- Continuous change: organisations are expected to continue the cycles of reflection and reorganisation, however changes may be both large and small and are likely to be interspersed with periods of stability.

Sherehiy and Karwowski[16] reported that more recent findings stress how enterprise agility is dependent on the workforce and that ultimately, without an agile workforce, agility cannot be achieved in an organisation. As jobs disaggregate and we need to coordinate human/machine interaction, we will have to figure out how we reassemble roles, tasks and structures. How roles relate and collaborate will be completely new. KPMG[17] and Swinburne[18] estimated that 85% of jobs that will exist in 2030 have not been invented yet. Work is transforming from being predictable, linear, mechanistic and siloed – where success is measured in terms of productive output – to being

---

15   Heerwagen, 2016.
16   Sherehiy & Karwowski, 2014.
17   KPMG, 2019.
18   Swinburne, 2019.

networked, collaborative, cross-functional and continuously changing. How work gets done, who does it, where it happens, how it is organised and even what work is – is all changing. Accenture[19] calls this new workforce the liquid workforce.

The right mix of people and machines in the workplace – and the implications not only for business but for wider society – is the critical talent question of our age. McKinsey[20] estimates that over 50% of current work activities are technically automatable and that 400-800 million individuals could be displaced and need to find new jobs by 2030. Tasks of many jobs can be broken down into separate, discrete pieces and can be disaggregated to different providers – this is the atomisation of work.[21] Clearly defined and repeatable tasks can be computerised – this is automation. When algorithms can analyse data faster and more accurately than humans, they can aid in our decision making – this is augmentation. This all means job redesign can create broader organisational and customer value, and interestingly, it actually creates more new jobs than it makes obsolete, with the caveat that the skill requirements are completely different. This is shown in Figure 1.2 below.

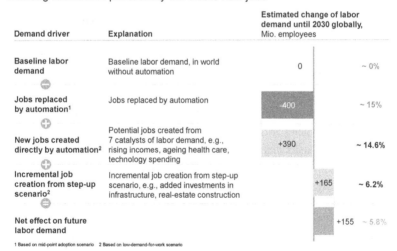

Figure 1.2: In the new world of work, there will be net increase of jobs[22]

---

19   Accenture, 2016.
20   McKinsey, 2018.
21   McGowan & Shipley, 2019.
22   Mercer, 2020.

These new jobs will require multiple and diverse skills that are different to the narrowly defined roles of the previous iterations of organisations. Work will be more cognitively complex, team based, collaborative and dependent on both technological competence and social skills, and less dependent on geography. There is a predicted net positive outlook for jobs and the future of work will, in fact, be more human. Talent can be utilised in a much more visible and interesting way as people can let go of the menial parts of their job and work on more complex and connected challenges. Work will be delivered through extended talent eco systems. Leaders can focus on coaching and developing people and taking care of organisational well-being. They can become more human centred while exploiting the best technology has to offer. People can work in smaller, multifunctional teams and learn a lot more from each other. Branson et al.[23] wrote that, "skills that differentiate human beings from machines, such as emotional intelligence, empathy, collaboration, advanced communication, leadership and problem solving, will become more prized".

Purpose as the key attractor

"Businesses today are finding that doing good also means doing well."[24]

The need for purpose is driven by global socio-economic factors seemingly beyond the control of corporations. But there is an upside – much of the discussion about purpose suggests that companies perform better if they have a clear sense of purpose. Purpose-driven companies make more money, have more engaged employees and more loyal customers, and are even better at innovation and transformational change. This link between purpose, authenticity and trust is important to emphasise if a company is to improve, not just safeguard, its performance and standing in the eyes of shareholders and society alike. A clear purpose based on human values – that is authentic and consistent with businesses' actions – is a foundation stone upon which reputation and performance are built.[25]

So what should a company's purpose be in the middle of COVID-19 when it is just trying to survive? Leading in a crisis is never easy, but hard times leave the most indelible imprints on a company's identity. Examine exactly

23   Branson et al., 2020, p. 3.
24   EY, 2018.
25   EY, 2018.

what is at stake for your employees, communities, customers, partners, and owners. All will have urgent, rapidly evolving needs that you should fully understand and prioritise. Some of these needs will be new and require creative thinking. Listen carefully to stakeholders that are well placed to inform you. Prepare for tension, too, as trade-offs arise among stakeholder groups, each with their own important needs.[26]

CASE STUDY: UNILEVER

Unilever's strategy is 'Purpose led, Future Fit'. They aim to prove that purpose-led brands, businesses and people deliver improved financial and societal impact by ensuring all their brands have a deeper and authentic societal and environmental purpose. Unilever strives to be a company that delivers on the trust consumers have in them and are building a sustainable and responsible future of work.

Unilever has thus developed a system anchored in the commitment that the organisation has a responsibility to generate and sustain employability, has a need to accelerate its own capabilities, and will meet these through increased investment and commitment to lifelong learning and by pioneering radical new forms of employment. This set of activities is called 'The Framework for the Future of Work'. The framework aims to deliver a purpose-driven, future-fit social contract of work for employees in a time of significant change, and to do so in a way that simultaneously enables business transformation.

The Unilever model is shown in Figure 1.3 below.

Figure 1.3: Unilever's "Purpose Led, Future Fit" model[27]

---

26   Shaninger, Zhang & Zhu, 2020.

27   Unilever, 2020.

CASE STUDY: NOVARTIS

108,000 associates at Novartis impact the lives of 799 million patients.

At Novartis, we are driven by our purpose. We reimagine medicine to improve and extend people's lives. We use innovative science and technology to address some of society's most challenging healthcare issues. We discover and develop breakthrough treatments and find new ways to deliver them to as many people as possible.

Our purpose provides a major source of inspiration for employees, and we constantly seek ways to show how their work contributes to its fulfilment. In 2019, Novartis' senior leaders increased communication about the impact we are having on global health – whether through the launch of innovative cell and gene therapies, or through our efforts to fight malaria. The company's purpose was a constant theme on our internal social media platform and intranet. We also held a series of live global events featuring external thought leaders to inspire employees with ideas from outside the organisation.[28]

With the onset of COVID-19, Novartis is making rapid progress in distributing the allocated USD 20 million of the Novartis COVID-19 Response Fund, announced mid-March, to impacted countries around the world. The fund aims to support public health initiatives designed to help communities manage the challenges posed by the pandemic, such as programmes to strengthen healthcare infrastructure, digital platforms for data collection or dissemination of important public health information, and community health programmes.[29]

Our products

70 billion doses of medicine touched the lives of 799 million patients in approximately 155 countries last year.

---

28   Novartis, 2020a.
29   Novartis, 2020b.

Our strategy

Our strategy is to build a leading, focused medicines company powered by advanced therapy platforms and data science. As we implement our strategy, we have five priorities to shape our future and help us continue to create value for our company, our shareholders and society. The strategic priorities are shown in Figure 1.4 below.

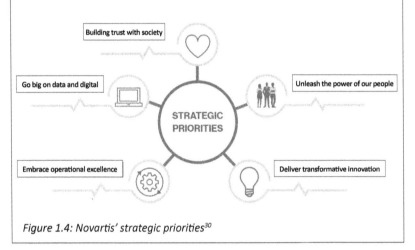

Figure 1.4: Novartis' strategic priorities[30]

Employees will need to adapt, reskill and upskill continuously

"As technology frees us to do different work, what are the mindsets, tools, and capabilities we need in order to embrace the value that humans can bring to work, and what types of investment does the organisation need to make to support that?"[31]

With the Fourth and Fifth Industrial Revolutions and the need for agility and digitalisation, the workforce needs to be future proofed. Employers are best placed to be at the vanguard of change and make a positive societal impact by upgrading the capabilities of their employees and equipping them with new skills. Employers themselves stand to reap the greatest benefit if they can successfully transform the workforce in this way.[32]

---

30   Novartis, 2020a.
31   Hagel, Schwartz & Wooll, 2019.
32   Hancock et al., 2020.

The workforce challenge for most companies is to make the transition from fixed work outcomes that deliver limited value to dynamic work outcomes with higher levels of potential value. In this shift, the workforce becomes key to value creation. The key is to redesign jobs to free up capacity for redefined work and to use automation or other technologies and workforce alternatives to perform rote work that prevents the workforce from spending more time on better understanding and addressing customer needs.

Integrating job redesign with work redefinition makes the goal of work a dynamic destination – one that expands both the financial value of the organisation and creates dynamic new sources of value and meaning for the customer, as shown in Figure 1.5 below.

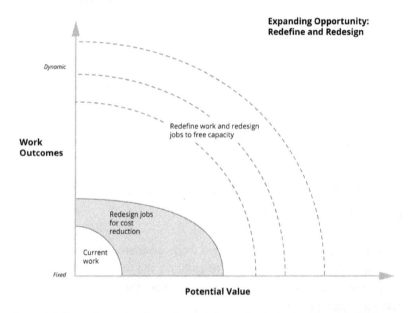

Figure 1.5: Expanding value through redefining and redesigning jobs and skills[33]

With the significant increase in virtual work, Dewhurst et al.[34] also remind us that in redefining jobs, companies should consider technological advances that make it easier to perform work remotely. Companies and employees today have more choices for where work is done and by whom. In cases where in-person interactions and sophisticated judgment are core to value delivery – performing medical procedures, sales, and giving financial advice

33   Hagel, Schwartz & Wooll, 2019.
34   Dewhurst et al., 2013.

fall into this category – the goal is to redesign the role so that people are spending all their time at the high end of their skill set.

HR needs to accelerate its transformation

"By managing the people implications of the 4IR for their organizations, HR leaders play a critical role in ensuring that businesses are able to successfully adopt and deploy new technologies – by supporting employees through adaptation and transition as their roles, tasks and skills change, and by integrating new worker and societal expectations to build attractive and inclusive workplaces."[35]

"The pandemic has forced the adoption of new ways of working. Organizations must reimagine their work and the role of offices in creating safe, productive, and enjoyable jobs and lives for employees."[36]

Ten Bulte[37] described the key HR practices to be impacted by Industry 4.0, i.e. organisations' design, staffing, performance management, training and education, and reward management. COVID-19 has accelerated remote and flexible work practices and employee safety and well-being practices. Organisational design will have to adapt to capability and value chain requirements, talent acquisition will use artificial intelligence and automation, performance management will use big data and be run on mobile phone apps, learning and development will have to ramped up as education and job requirements become increasingly mismatched, and rewards and benefits will become more individualised. Static workforces organised around specific skills and functions will need to transform into adaptable workforces organised around projects. These shifts will necessitate the reinvention of the HR function to a strategic, agile and digitally- and data-enabled function.

Human Resource professionals will have the task of leading the workforce and capability transition and build the capabilities for the future. They will drive the "humanisation" of the organisation and the adaptability of its leaders and culture. They will have to help the organisation rethink what people can do and will use data and analytics to do so.

---

35   World Economic Forum White Paper, 2019.

36   Boland et al., 2020.

37   Ten Bulte, 2018.

With the growth of disruption and 'always on' working, HR must balance the need to help organisations grow new sources of revenue AND assist employees with their well-being.[38] However, "HR departments are currently undertrained, underequipped and insufficiently experienced to drive the development of such organizations. In some cases, HR may be culturally removed or even hostile to such solutions. Human resources must inevitably work with professional communities to develop new organizational transformation and design capabilities to design and implement leaner and more agile organizations."[39]

☑ Checklist

1. How has the convergence of Fourth Industrial Revolution technologies in the midst of the pandemic, job market disruptions to both remote work and work requiring physical presence, and a wide-ranging call for greater inclusivity, equity and social justice affected your organisation?

2. How are you adjusting your organisation to the virtual age?

3. How clear is your purpose to all your stakeholders?

4. Have you updated your operating model, organisational design and critical capabilities to be relevant in the future of work in your organisation?

5. Will your organisation be able to learn, adapt and innovate faster than its competition?

6. Will your organisation be able to create an environment that enables and promotes the highest levels of human development, human engagement, and human excellence in critical thinking, creativity and innovation?

7. Will your organisation be able to attract, develop, and retain the best human learners, thinkers and collaborators?

8. How adaptive is your HR function to all of these changes?

---

38 Dussert, 2014.
39 Orange, 2016, p.19.

CHAPTER 2

People Strategy for the new world of work

In this chapter, the need for strong People Strategies that drive organisational sustainability and key people imperatives that drive agility and capability is assessed. There is a particular focus on the need for a wholesale redesign of work and skills in all industries and jobs, as mentioned before.

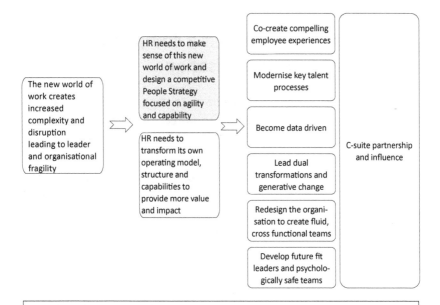

Key ideas

- A great People Strategy is a competitive advantage for an organisation.
- Key new people imperatives are needed for the new world of work.
- A wholesale redesign of work and skills is required.
- COVID-19 and social change has impacted People Priorities.

"The digital revolution is a human revolution. While new technologies are what's driving the Fourth Industrial Revolution, ultimately, it is people who will bring it to life in businesses. As HR Leaders, we play a pivotal role in helping to lead our organizations to a new future of work – one that has the potential to be more inclusive, more purposeful and one which can deliver more positive impact to our people and our consumers. It is for this reason why I think there's no better time to be in HR."[40]

"As we move deeper into the Fourth Industrial Revolution (4IR), we clearly see HR changing to reflect our role as a crucial business driver. Our success in the future of work will depend heavily on our ability to effectively prepare our workforce – by fostering a culture of reskilling, upskilling and lifelong learning."[41]

A great People Strategy is a competitive advantage for an organisation

As business strategies undergo a fundamental re-think, so must organisations' People Strategies. True competitive advantage comes from the people in the organisation, but to achieve this, you need a clearly differentiated People Strategy that is business-, customer- and human-centric. Organisations that can leverage talent and energy can outperform their competitors and achieve sustained growth. As Mercer[42] stated: "Thriving organisations treat their workforce as an asset in which to invest – not simply a business cost." Companies with a strong and effective People Strategy have a CEO who cares about People Strategy and an HR executive who is a close confidante of the CEO.

The People Strategy team needs a deep understanding of overall business economics and a broad perspective on how People Strategies can drive business strategy and boost performance. Kevin Green[43] wrote that successful companies have a great customer offering and a world class employee experience, and it is the combination of the two that creates competitive advantage. The design of People Strategy, initiatives, work redesign and plans needs to be, at its core, based on human centred design, neuroscience and behaviour-based insights. Rather than just asking people

---

40   Nair, 2019.
41   World Economic Forum, 2019.
42   Mercer, 2020.
43   Green, 2019.

what they need, or assuming we know what they need, organisations are now paying much more interest to how the people they interact with actually behave.

BCG[44] wrote that the process of defining People Strategy requires honesty concerning such issues as moving manufacturing offshore or recognising deficits in leadership, succession planning, employee skills, and diversity of gender, age, ethnicity and culture. They proposed that because People Strategy critically influences business strategy, line managers need to do more than just manage employees; they need to be deeply involved in People Strategy, and the HR department needs to be deeply involved in business strategy. In recognition of this interdependent relationship, best-practice companies are increasingly rotating executives between HR and business units.

People Strategy is not just about strategy but also about implementation. People plans should be developed and monitored with the same care as financial plans, consuming at least one-fifth of a company's overall planning time. Because the people plan and the business plan should dovetail, the former should remain a work in progress until executives know that the latter is achievable. Best-practice companies deploy scorecards that translate people goals into individual management objectives. For example, Repsol YPF, an integrated oil and gas company, has set up an HR committee that includes key members of the executive committee and is led by the chairman and chief executive. The chairman and his top management team use individual scorecards to plan and track each manager's initiatives relating to such targeted areas as employee development, accountability, entrepreneurship, collaboration, and recognition.

MERCER PEOPLE STRATEGY METHODOLOGY

Mercer proposes five components of an effective People Strategy.

1.   Align vision.
2.   Define the future
3.   Determine strategy
4.   Design solutions
5.   Drive performance.

---

44   BCG, 2006.

Start by understanding the external causes of change and the trends and understand how the business will move forward and grow future revenues. When defining the future, workforce planning beyond the traditional approach is critical. Businesses need to think through what they need versus what they have. Rather than conducting granular, job-based forecasting, companies need to think about organisational capaability, leadership, and critical roles, and then ask what skills and knowhow they need in those roles to target the strategy appropriately. The next phase is design solutions, essential to identify the few and HR must align on key staffing principles such as what they need to attract talent and use the talent ecosystem, how/what they will develop and about what culture and leadership is needed.[45]

Start by understanding the external causes of change and the trends, and understand how the business will move forward and grow future revenues. When defining the future, workforce planning beyond the traditional approach is critical. Businesses need to think through what they need versus what they have. Rather than conducting granular, job-based forecasting, companies need to think about organisational capability, leadership and critical roles, and then ask what skills and know-how they need in those roles to target the strategy appropriately. The next phase is to design people solutions that will drive sustainable performance.[46]

Key new people imperatives are needed for the new world of work

What should the focus be of these People Strategies in the new world of work? In their HR 4.0 White Paper[47], the World Economic Forum identified six key imperatives that business leaders, partnering with their human resources counterparts, will need to implement:

1. *Develop new leadership capabilities for the 4IR (Fourth Industrial Revolution):* as organisations operate more distributed business models, leaders will need to lead from the edge, adopt the right

---

45   Mercer, 2020.

46   Mercer, 2020.

47   World Economic Forum, 2019.

technologies, drive a new vision of organisational culture, and shape innovative People Strategies for the future of work.

2. *Manage the integration of technology in the workplace:* the way work gets done is changing. A growing area of responsibility for HR is to partner with CEOs and C-suite leaders to achieve the optimal combination of human workforce and automation to ensure a positive impact on the future of work.

3. *Enhance the employee experience:* the increasing complexity of the workforce and the use of technology is calling for a change in the way work is experienced. HR plays a vital role in defining, measuring and enabling the meaningful employee experience in the 4IR.

4. *Build an agile and personalised learning culture:* HR plays a leading role in fostering a culture of lifelong learning in the context of declining demand for certain skills, the emergence of new ones, and the requirement for talent to continuously learn, unlearn and relearn.

5. *Establishing metrics for valuing human capital:* the mutually beneficial relationship between the workforce, organisations and society make it essential for HR to create a compelling case for establishing viable and scalable measures of human capital as a key performance driver, and continuously demonstrate the impact of its work on business performance.

6. *Embedding diversity and inclusion:* changing social, economic and political forces bring an opportunity for organisations to profoundly advance inclusion and diversity. HR plays a pivotal role in promoting a sense of purpose and belonging in the workforce, and equality and prosperity for the communities and regions in which they operate.

The Deloitte 2020 Human Capital trends survey is explicit about the shift in outcomes for HR, as is shown in Table 2.1 below.

Table 2.1: HR Outcomes: Shifting from today to tomorrow[48]

HR outcomes: Shifting from today to tomorrow

Area of impact	Today's outcome	Tomorrow's outcome
Building leadership skills	Building leaders with the skills required to fill current leadership pipeline roles	Building leadership teams and capabilities for future and unknown opportunities that can lead through ambiguity and operate with an enterprise and ecosystem mindset
Upskilling the workforce	Delivering skills-based learning programmes for critical workforce segments	Curating personalised and team-based learning experiences that build sustained capabilities relevant to the organisation and broader ecosystem
Promoting teaming and agility	Experimenting with the use of teams across an established (often hierarchical or matrixed organisational structure	Embedding collaborative ways of working across the enterprise and the ecosystem, making teams the core unit of analysis and action for performance and management
Developing the workforce experience and brand	Implementing targeted employee experience programs focused on reinforcing the internal workforce brand	Designing an end-to-end human experience that integrates both the workforce and customer perspectives both internally and externally
Accessing new capabilities	Hiring new talent in accordance with business demand	Creating on-demand access to capabilities (human or machine) across the enterprise and the ecosystem
Integrating automation in the way work gets done	Introducing digital tools to increase the efficiency and effectiveness of HR-specific processes	Digitising the flow of work across the organisation
Defining and promoting the organisation's purpose	Crafting and reinforcing mission and value statements/principles	Engaging the workforce in continuously reimagining work to tie purpose to meaning – personal, organisational, and societal

All of these initiatives have to support the organisation's road to Agile. Table 2.2 highlights some key HR imperatives from KPMG's research that drive agility, which should be considered in People Strategy.

---

48   Deloitte, 2020.

Table 2.2: HR imperatives to drive agility in organisations[49]

1	Program focus to outcome focus	HR function to be more outcome oriented and not just focus on execution and design of programmes. Any HR intervention that is designed needs to have a strong linkage to business performance. The role of the HR function to become far more evolved and be a driver of business performance and not just an enabler.
2	Alignment to purpose	Keeping the larger purpose of the organisation intact is a key role of HR in agile organisations. Clarifying and communication of the purpose will be a key differentiator as compared to designing a strong employee value proposition. In an agile environment self-operating teams are to be given greater autonomy and power. The teams need to be bound together through one common purpose.
3	Creating a compelling experience	It is critical to look at employee experience as a whole as supposed to designing employee engagement interventions which address a specific need and requirement.
4	Actualise culture	HR process and practices to re-inforce the culture of the organisation. Making real-time feedback a reality and encouraging collaboration within and outside teams will be critical.
5	Reward for prominence	Agile organisations are driven by power of teams. Rewards and incentive structures to be centered on team performance and collaborative solutioning.

People Strategy also has to support the digital transformation of an organisation. Digital transformation includes the optimal inclusion of big data, cognitive augmentation, and the use of advanced analytics that help in driving value across the organisation. This transformation has pushed the HR function to take on new responsibilities. Digital technologies will drive interactions within and outside the organisation going forward. The journey starts with developing technological and digital capabilities within the HR function and harnessing the potential of the same to drive key outcomes. KPMG[50] listed key HR imperatives for a new digital journey, as per Table 2.3.

---

49   KPMG, 2018.
50   KPMG, 2018.

Table 2.3: HR imperatives for the digital journey[51]

1	Focus on the problem first	• Utilise design thinking, taking an outside-in approach that focuses on customers and users and their specific needs. • Combining business knowledge with an innovative methodology to deliver solutions that are aligned with the business, defined by humanity and refined by analytics.
2	Design for people, not processes	• Look beyond technology and focus on meaningful interactions between people and processes to imagine what's possible. • Develop user personas to understand desires, motivations and experiences. • Influence behaviours to align to business strategies.
3	Deliver small, fast and often	• Foster and embrace a culture of continuous improvement that drives the entire organisation. • Focus on stakeholder needs to inform feature development. • Test hypotheses and quickly refine them, connecting user motivations to business outcomes.
4	Always look for improvements	• Look to cultural shifts as they catalyst for wider organisational change. • Provide design and architecture for solutions that are future-ready. • Used evidence-based approach to improve solutions based on market trends and impacts.

CASE STUDY: VOLSKWAGEN[52]

After the scandal in 2015, Volkswagen renewed its strategy, TOGETHER, and added a renewed focus on people. With the new human resources strategy "Empower to transform", the Group is continuing with key and successful approaches of its human resource management. These include the pronounced stakeholder focus in corporate governance, comprehensive participation rights for employees, outstanding training opportunities, the principle of long term service through systematic

---

51   KPMG, 2018.
52   Volkswagen, 2017.

employee retention and the aspiration to appropriately balance performance and remuneration. At the same time, the new human resources strategy is setting innovative trends. Hierarchies are being dismantled and modern forms of working such as agile working – whereby most responsibility for the work organisation is transferred to the teams – are set to be expanded. In the future, cooperating robots will ease heavy physical work in factories and digital processes will simplify administration.

The company's human resources strategy is based on five overarching objectives:

1. The Volkswagen Group aims to be an excellent employer with all of its brands and companies worldwide.

2. Highly competent and dedicated employees strive for excellence in terms of innovation, added value and customer focus.

3. A sustainable work organisation ensures optimal working conditions in factories and offices.

4. An exemplary corporate culture creates an open work climate that is characterised by mutual trust and collaboration.

5. The company's human resources work is highly employee-oriented while also aiming for operational excellence and providing strategic value-added contributions.

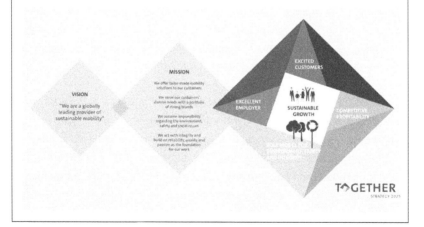

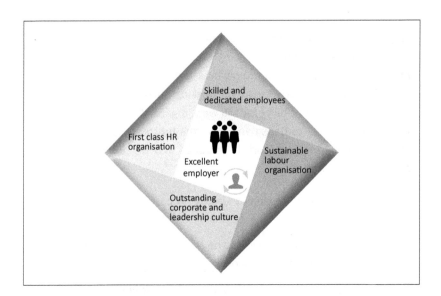

CASE STUDY: ADIDAS

Adidas launched its new strategy, 'Creating the New', in 2015, based on the three pillars of speed, key cities and open source. In terms of people, Adidas states:

At Adidas, we believe that our people are the key to the company's success. Their performance, well-being and knowledge have a significant impact on brand desire, consumer satisfaction and, ultimately, our financial performance. Through the delivery of our People Strategy, we focus our efforts on four fundamentals: the attraction and retention of the right talents, role model leadership, diversity and inclusion, as well as the creation of a unique corporate culture.

The People Strategy consists of four pillars that serve as a basis for creating the culture and environment for their people in order to successfully support 'Creating the New'. These four pillars also serve as a tool for prioritisation, sense-checking and measuring their HR actions and initiatives. The People Strategy is implemented through a portfolio of projects which will directly deliver into each of the four pillars. They use two people KPIs: employee experience (NPS) as an internal measure and employer rankings as an external measure.

People Strategy			
Defines and inspires the right organizational culture for 'Creating the New'			
Attraction and retention of the right talents	**Role model leadership**	**Diversity and inclusion**	**Culture**
Meaningful reasons to join and stay	**Role models who inspire us**	**Bring forward fresh and diverse perspectives**	**A creative climate to make a difference**
Attract and retain great talent by offering personal experiences, choices and individual careers.	Inspire and nurture role model leadership.	Represent and live the diversity of our consumers in our people.	It is our goal to develop a culture that cherishes creativity, collaboration and confidence – three behaviors we deem crucial to the successful delivery of our corporate strategy.

In 2019, Adidas continued to roll out a new HR cloud-based system platform that aims to further enhance the HR system landscape by driving standardisation, digitisation and automation of currently potentially time-consuming processes across all HR areas. This will allow the HR function to proactively manage the workforce, improve the employee experience, and enable the entire organisation to make more data-driven decisions.

After successful consolidation of their HR Shared Services in 2019 into a cross-functional global business service, Global Business Services (GBS), operation centers are currently set up in Porto, Dalian and Portland. All employee queries related to topics of an administrative nature, such as compensation, benefits, time management and HR systems, are centrally channelled and managed through GBS. As a result, their HR Partners are enabled to fully focus on their core business, supporting line managers and employees on strategic topics such as career counselling, people management and coaching.

Adidas puts a specific focus on recruiting what it called 'creators' and nurturing partnerships with creative individuals. Steve Fogarty, who leads the Global Talent Futures Team at Adidas, notes, 'We were taking a stand as an organisation, to put creativity at the top. Our consumers and our talent are creators. Creators don't want to be dictated to but express themselves to the world through their uniqueness and creativity.'

Adidas needed to recruit 4,000 – 6,000 creators a year, as well as keep and nurture the creativity of the people it already has. To this end, it has a clear statement about its brand and provides employees and partners with the space and support to make real contributions. However, what makes the process work so well, is that Adidas has aligned its People Strategy with its business strategy and worked to build a culture that gives emphasis to the central role of creativity. This is something that Fathima Saleem and Oriol Iglesias emphasise when they note that successful internal branding is a company- wide effort, which requires a supportive culture that integrates 'brand ideologies, leadership, human resource management, internal brand communications, and internal brand communities, to enable employees to consistently co-create brand value with multiple stakeholders.'

The company now gets 800,000 applications a year. As Fogarty argues, 'We have seen our engagement levels go up across our social channels and we've seen the performance of our organisation's talent continue to rise.' That, in turn, has fed through to a succession of innovative product ranges including NMD and Yeezy, as well as the revitalisation of Stan Smiths and Superstars (the best-selling shoes in the world in 2015 and 2016). In 2016, Adidas's global revenue grew by 18% and net income by 21%, while in its key North American territory, sales grew by 31% in the first quarter of 2017. The performance is a testament to both thinking and 'doing strategy'.[53, 54]

CASE STUDY: NOVARTIS

Unleash the power of our people

To help us fulfil our company purpose of reimagining medicine, we are changing the way we work to unleash the talent and creativity of our people. We made progress in 2019 on our cultural transformation, which is a strategic priority for Novartis. We aim to make our culture a driver of innovation, performance and reputation, and a source of sustainable competitive advantage. Cultural transformation means ensuring employees feel **inspired** by our purpose. We want them to be constantly **curious** about new ideas that can improve health outcomes

---

53   Ind, 2019.
54   Adidas, 2019.

for patients, physicians and society as a whole. And we strive to create an **"unbossed"** culture in which leaders are encouraged to serve their teams, remove obstacles, and empower people to attain their personal and professional ambitions. To support this transformation, our goal is to attract, develop and promote highly talented people who embody the new culture, and to build a diverse and inclusive workforce so we can tap the broadest possible range of skills, experiences and backgrounds.[55]

COVID-19 has changed People Priorities

"With the rapidly evolving COVID-19 pandemic, leaders find themselves managing a dynamic and uncertain workforce supply and demand. What is clear is that the short term will be challenging. Temporary workforce reductions are already occurring, and more are sure to come."[56]

COVID-19 brought a wide range of discussions about work and accelerated change. Strack et al.[57] defined some People Priorities for the 'New Now' that are worth considering:

1. Smart work will become the new normal: virtual collaboration and remote work will be scaled on a more permanent basis and mixed models will emerge that mix onsite and remote work.

2. Physical and mental health will be more important: standards of corporate hygiene will be raised and big data and digital tools like apps will promote social distancing, track infections and be used for other health issues. Mental health and mindfulness will become even more important than before. Focus will be placed on developing resilience.

3. New paradigms for skills and talent will emerge: an adaptive learning ecosystem will be needed that integrates reflection, learning and innovation. Before the crisis, it was estimated that 60% of the workforce would need reskilling in the coming years, but now the timeline for this has been accelerated. Digital savvy will be a key skill for everyone.

4. Flexible workforces will accelerate: alternate employment models will escalate and fluctuations in supply and demand will be simulated more

55 Novartis, 2019.
56 Deloitte, 2020b.
57 Strack et al., 2020.

proactively and frequently. Workspace, work time and affiliation (full time, contract, freelancer) will all be considered, which will impact performance and reward systems.

5. Leadership will become more human: leaders will lead with more empathy, transparency and direction than before and they will listen to employees more.

6. Culture will become more purpose driven and resilient: purpose, vision and values will have to be more aligned, and sustainability and social impact considered, in order to attract and keep the best talent.

Deloitte[58] has proposed the following People Strategies in the short to medium term:

*   A strategic talent review understanding the segments where there is currently high and low demand, and balancing the short and long term views to optimise talent.

*   Accelerate plans for new ways of working and taking the organisation digital. Consider which workforce segments can work virtually on a permanent basis and on a 'gig' employment basis.

*   Implement options to temporarily reduce the workforce and provide more flexibility for the business to deal with short term pressures.

✎ Checklist

1. Across value chains within your business, how are changes in technology and business models likely to affect work styles, jobs and skills?

2. What is the gap between current capabilities and job types, and those of the future? Which will disappear? Which will appear? Which will change?

3. Which roles are strategic and core to the business? Which are candidates for non-traditional work forms such as automation?

4. Which skills do people need that they do not have today? What is your plan for upskilling and reskilling them?

---

58   Deloitte, 2020b.

5. How well does your current learning approach meet future content and delivery needs, and what role does leadership play?

6. In which areas is it sensible and desirable for work to be done "outside" your physical or legal borders? Where are emerging talent pools for these kinds of tasks located? Who are they?

7. What characteristics do future leaders need to display? What is the desired mix of technical and behavioural skills in your leaders?

8. How do you cultivate the right employer value proposition (EVP) for your people? What is the right mix of reward and non-reward benefits (such as flexible working, health benefits and competitive pensions) that will attract, motivate and retain different talent segments?

9. Is your culture driving the right behaviours and do you have the right culture to manage the changes ahead?

10. How do you ensure people can thrive at work? Are they enabled to excel in their work and their career? Are they healthy, energised and productive?

11. How are you responding to the COVID crisis?

CHAPTER 3

Futureproof your HR Operating Model, Structure and Capabilities

This chapter follows on from the context of the future of work and the People Strategies relevant for this new context, and describes how to futureproof the Human Resource Operating Model, Structure and Capabilities.

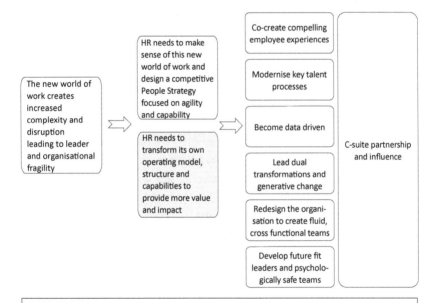

Key ideas

- HR functions have a credibility and impact problem.
- HR MUST become a critical driver of agility and capability.
- It is time to move beyond the Ulrich model.
- HR capabilities need to change fundamentally.

HR functions have a credibility and impact problem

"Our point of view is that we need to stop refining concepts for HR that were designed for the world of today and yesterday. The world of tomorrow is going to be so much different, that current concepts (that very often are not effective today) will be misaligned in the world of tomorrow. And if we keep refining them, our profession will become increasingly irrelevant. We do not need an evolution; we will need a disruptive revolution or re-imagination of our profession to stay relevant for the years to come."[59]

"The HR function has to make smart choices about the trade-offs required. Accelerating HR transformation is needed today, but so too are businesses' cost containment measures. Which investments in HR transformation, such as digitalization, are priorities to bring forward? Which HR efforts can be paused without detriment to the business' ability to rebound post-pandemic?"[60]

HR is an evolving profession. One of the core missions of HR in the coming years will likely involve establishing more flexible organisations and forms of employment. However, HR departments are currently undertrained, underequipped and insufficiently experienced to drive the development of such organisations. In some cases, HR may be culturally removed or even hostile to such solutions.[61] Why is this so?

Most of the models used by HR currently were developed in a different time over 20 years ago, and HR has struggled to loosen themselves from the manual and rigid processes they have been following for so long. I am currently involved in several organisational and HR transformations and thought it timely to reflect on some real challenges HR professionals face in the field. Firstly, there is the challenge of having to transform the organisation while being transformed yourself. This requires an exceptional ability to be on the balcony and dance floor at the same time – simultaneously detached and connected. The second key challenge is the lack of data or different data sources, which leads to an inability to do meaningful people and talent

---

59   KennedyFitch, 2019.
60   Mercer, 2020.
61   Orange, 2016.

analytics as prescribed to help identify the key levers and business impacts HR can focus on. In the third instance, it is the capability gaps of the HR teams themselves. Most of the time the key gaps we identify in the work sessions are collaboration across silos, analytics expertise and customer centricity. The fourth key issue is that of increased pressure on HR to show value add and impact, while being highly responsive. This has been brewing for some time but has now become absolutely critical. HR needs to be 100% aligned to business priorities, human centric and agile to adapt to changing priorities.

Gemini[62] argued that it is time to blow up HR. Their argument is that there is a lack of strategic systemic and agile thinking coming from the HR teams at a time when leaders need guidance in the uncertainty they are facing; they do not need more processes, policies or more restructures – they need new mindsets and capabilities, as well as innovative, cross-functional ideas. In fact:

- HR has become too remote and impersonal: it is not employee experience driven and employees feel HR does not really care about them – the rhetoric and the actions do not measure up.

- HR has not been seen to courageously stand up for employees in an era of high levels of engagement and incivility: people feel they get nowhere when they ask for help from HR.

"Time is of the essence and today's HR leaders need to be initiating and sustaining "the right conversations with business leaders", explained Johanna Söderström, SVP HR at The Dow Chemical Company. "HR teams need to become 'comfortable being uncomfortable' in today's disrupted environment."[63]

HR MUST become a critical driver of agility and capability

"To support this new kind of work and the evolving and diverse workforce, HR now must be a digital partner, talent driver and key strategic partner contributing to the business agenda. The focus of HR is moving toward

---

62   Gemini, 2018.
63   KPMG, 2019.

customised, agile solutions to digitally transform the business – creating engaging workforce experiences while catering to the needs of the enterprise."[64]

HR must take on the challenge of reshaping itself to become a critical partner in agility; wait and see will not do. The future of HR is now if it transforms to a connected, digital and engaged function and reshapes organisations around nimble and responsive talent. HR has to speak the language of the business and focus on how to grow the business, improve profitability, and create responsiveness to changing environments. It needs to be seen as a function that is taking the lead on understanding what makes people tick, as well as what culture helps people and organisations thrive so that we create places of work that are a true augmentation of human capability with technology.[65]

Accenture[66] shows the changing nature of the work and workforces and how it impacts HR in Figure 3.1 below.

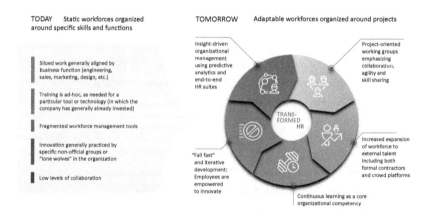

Figure 3.1: The changing nature of work and workforce

KPMG[67] sees it as a 4-step journey:

1.   Align the HR architecture to the business value drivers.

2.   Support agility through strategy and structure.

64   Accenture, 2017.
65   KPMG, 2019.
66   Accenture, 2017.
67   KPMG, 2018.

3. Own the digital agenda.

4. Build capabilities for the future.

The Deloitte 2020 Global Human Capital Trends survey also outlined a few key actions for HR[68]:

- Increase new capabilities and adopt a new mindset for the digital age.

- Change the HR organisation design to incorporate agile and team-based work that flexes based on business needs.

- Increase the efficiency through which HR activities occur through automation and simplified employee experiences.

- Expand the expectations and stature of HR leaders by elevating focus, impact and value.

It is time to move beyond the Ulrich model

Accenture[69] commented that to help an entire organisation become nimbler, the HR organisation itself will have to become nimble as well, i.e. it will need to apply many of the practices it prescribes to the entire workforce to itself – such as continual learning and new ways of structuring work that break down silos. To adopt such a model, HR professionals themselves may have fluid jobs and may need to develop new organisational structures that enable more flexibility than today's standard organisational model allows. The new HR function must start to be more project based, agile and digitally enabled, all while reducing operating costs.

The Ulrich model, which is widely used, needs to be transformed into a model that is digitally driven, processes that are automated, and a function driven by data, analytics and human centred design.[70] It also needs to be much more agile and fluid in order to respond to changing business priorities. Francine Katsoudas, chief people officer at Cisco, had to 'break HR' to move from a 'one size fits all' to a 'one size fits one' approach, through a 25-hour 'breakathon'. The panel agreed that organisations need to enable decisions on the basis of knowledge rather than hierarchy, and that the role

---

68   Deloitte, 2020.
69   Accenture, 2017.
70   Ulrich, 1996.

of an organisation's culture is to let talent flow to where it can have the greatest impact. The art is to find a balance between having control, stifling innovation and total chaos.

Deloitte proposed a new High-Impact Operating Model for HR in the new world of work, which places the employee and leadership customers at the centre. "The High-Impact HR Operating Model empowers business leaders, employees, and HR professionals by aligning the work an organisation needs with the capabilities that can deliver it most effectively. It emphasizes coordination within and beyond HR. It reshapes the roles and responsibilities within HR and the ways HR interacts inside and beyond the enterprise's walls. It incorporates technology as another 'role' in the operating model to create an integrated experience for the HR customer."[71] This model is shown in Figure 3.2 below.

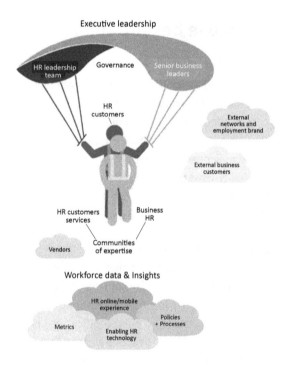

Figure 3.2: The High Impact HR Operating Model[72]

---

71   Deloitte, 2014.
72   Deloitte, 2014.

---

a. Transitioning from "centres" of expertise (CoEs) to "communities" of expertise or practice

The most important role of CoEs is to further business strategy through people and to create community and connections across the entire eco system. The COE has to use design thinking and manage a portfolio of solutions, and needs to leverage technology and use data and analytics insights when designing fit for purpose solutions.[73] EY[74] concurred that today's CoEs are too one-dimensional and disconnected, arguing that they need to evolve into Communities of Expertise and Practice (CoE/CoP). According to EY, they need to facilitate networking across traditional organisational boundaries and drive connections with individuals who may not typically interact on a regular basis. CoPs will deliver strategic insights with business partners/ advisors, in conjunction with educating business on People Strategies.

b. Business Partners/Advisors

EY[75] sees the role of a business advisor as being multi-faceted and playing a critical strategic role in a business. They will be critical thinkers, focused on proactive problem solving and solutions for People Strategy, leadership development, coaching, mentoring, talent deployment and digital workforce engagement, as well as risk advisors for the business. Some of the best business advisors may come from the business in the form of rotational assignments to the people (HR) function.

Bafaro et al.[76] wrote that HR business partners need to stop acting as HR generalists and show that they really drive the critical talent and capability set and their performance, engagement and well-being. In addition, they should be held accountable for year-on-year capability development and gaps, engagement and attrition, and their work and advice should be based on analytics and insights against key business priorities and measures. Many organisations now cross-skill line managers for these roles. Eileen Naughton, for example, stepped in to run people operations at Google from her role as managing director and vice president of sales and operations in the United Kingdom and Ireland. PepsiCo has also begun to fill some HR roles with people from engineering, technology and process-oriented backgrounds;

---

73   Deloitte, 2018.
74   Zeolli et al., 2017.
75   Zeolli et al., 2017.
76   Bafaro et al., 2017.

leaders at the soft drink giant say that engaging the business with data is critical to expanding the strategic role of HR.

HR business partners and communities of expertise (CoEs) should work together as a business focused internal consultancy. Business partners form the vertical "go to market" account management/project management/ change management team, while the CoEs form the horizontal expert teams (SWOT teams) as shown in Figure 3.3. Business decides what the critical projects and strategic capabilities are that need to be developed, which become the scope of work for the team. For CoEs, this means alignment to critical business challenges and a focus on solution design and delivery. This model can only work if the people services/administration team supports the day-to-day HR requirements of the business effectively.[77]

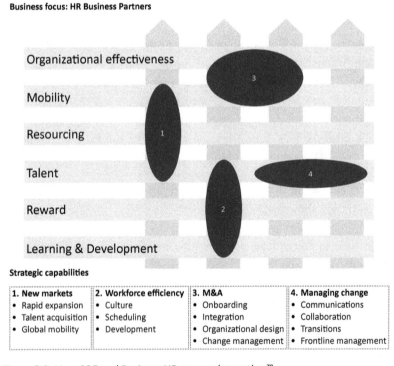

Business focus: HR Business Partners

Organizational effectiveness

Mobility

Resourcing

Talent

Reward

Learning & Development

Strategic capabilities

1. New markets	2. Workforce efficiency	3. M&A	4. Managing change
• Rapid expansion	• Culture	• Onboarding	• Communications
• Talent acquisition	• Scheduling	• Integration	• Collaboration
• Global mobility	• Development	• Organizational design	• Transitions
		• Change management	• Frontline management

Figure 3.3: How COE and Business HR can work together[78]

---

77 Deloitte, 2018.

78 Deloitte, 2013.

c. Operational services to people services and even Employee Experience Team

The current HR operations team is also undergoing a fundamental change. EY sees this team as People Solution and Services, explaining that this team reengineers and automates HR processes, creating digital and artificial intelligence solutions for people processes and decision making. KPMG[79] concurs that automating high-volume, repetitive, rules-based tasks using digital labour will free up employees to focus on work that is more strategic and of higher value to the overall business. And with machines needing less supervision and oversight, management will also be free to increase its focus on business efficiency, performance and competitiveness – including customer service.

To reduce overall call volume and the number of People Solution front line associates, case management solutions offer employees direct access to services by submitting tickets without any human interaction. Click to chat applications and chatbots, prevalent on many consumer product sites, is an essential service to further reduce service ticket volume by answering customer inquiries in real-time. Employees' direct access to click to chat and a digital workforce will soon be the base level standard for an employee's experience with their People Services teams.

CASE STUDY: BBVA

BBVA is a customer-centric global financial services group founded in 1857. The Group has a strong leadership position in the Spanish market, is the largest financial institution in Mexico, it has leading franchises in South America and the Sunbelt Region of the United States. It is also the leading shareholder in Turkey's Garanti BBVA. Its purpose is to bring the age of opportunities to everyone, based on their customers' real needs: provide the best solutions, helping them make the best financial decisions, through an easy and convenient experience. The institution rests in solid values: Customer comes first, we think big and we are one team. Its responsible banking model aspires to achieve a more inclusive and sustainable society.

---

79   KPMG, 2019.

BBVA reorganised their Talent and Culture team of 2000 people in 10 countries under a fully Agile organisation and governance model into four different groups:

1º – Front:
- Team of business partners offering strategic advice and support to internal customers: areas, managers and employees. Business partners have to play a strategic and proactive role in giving service to internal areas, based on a very good knowledge of their needs and priorities. They also have to act as coaches for managers and as a point of contact for employees through their life cycle in the organization. They typically represent 10-15% of the team.

2º- Disciplines:
- Expert teams with the role of defining the strategy and developing the models, policies, tools and platforms for their respective areas of expertise (such as talent management, compensation and benefits, internal communication, organization...) They ensure connectivity of people in execution teams through global Communities of Practice in which practitioners in their field share knowledge and best practices and even co-create new models and platforms. Discipline teams are typically senior but very small (just 2-3 people by discipline), representing no more than 10-15% of the total team.

3º – Solutions Development:
- Pool of professionals fully dedicated to executing projects or build new solutions following scrum principles. They constitute multidisciplinary teams with autonomy to organize their work and end-to-end accountability and capacity to execute. These scrum teams typically work in 2-3-week sprints following an iterative, incremental process to continuously learn from (internal) customer feedback. They are dynamically assigned, on a quarterly basis, to the evolving strategic priorities of the area through a staffing process. Ideally, they should represent at least 25-30% of the team.

4º – Employee Experience
- Group of teams empowered to execute all end-to-end processes in the function and deliver value to internal customers using Kanban. They have a big impact in employee experience, operational excellence and productivity. By concentrating all processes which were previously fragmented into different units, there is a clear opportunity to stop doing things that do not add significant value, apply process engineering to redesign processes for better quality and efficiency, and apply automation, robotics and machine learning techniques to raise productivity. Furthermore, we can define a catalogue of services to be provided to internal customers, linked to specific KPIs and service level agreements so we can measure and continuously improve quality of service. These teams normally represent 40-50% of the area.[80]

CASE STUDY: ING

ING is a global bank with a strong European base. Our 53,000 employees serve around 38.4 million customers, corporate clients and financial institutions in over 40 countries. Our purpose is to empower people to stay a step ahead in life and in business. Our products include savings, payments, investments, loans and mortgages in most of our retail markets. For our Wholesale Banking clients we provide specialised lending, tailored corporate finance, debt and equity market solutions, payments & cash management and trade and treasury services. Customer experience is what differentiates us and we're continuously innovating to improve it. We also partner with others to bring disruptive ideas to market faster.

ING's HR organization, like that of many companies, is built on three pillars. Reorganising these pillars using agile allowed HR to work more efficiently and create more consistent – yet still high-quality – products and services, with fewer staff and fewer handovers. The pillars today work in an integrated way to deliver HR's purpose: building the craftsmanship and the engagement of everyone who works at ING, so they can deliver on the purpose and the strategy of the bank.

---

80   BBVA, 2020.

HR Business Partners

HRBPs advance the People Strategy throughout the business. A dozen individual HRBPs have their own accounts – senior management, leaders of tribes and communities of expertise (CoE) – and are responsible for driving the people agenda of these groups.

The rest of the HRBPs make up a flexible pool of partners who work primarily on execution-based teams (so-called to emphasize action) modelled loosely upon the delivery organization's squads. Each of these "impact teams" is dedicated to one area: for instance, one is executing the bank's new Step-Up Performance Management program; another is implementing ING's new ways of working in other parts of the bank. This flexible pool enables HR to prioritize how it assigns resources, to ensure standardised products and services, and to develop and implement new tools and processes in far less time than it once took. The model allows ING to allocate resources where their impact will be greatest.

People Services

This group, which provides day-to-day services to employees, is modelled along the lines of the call centre teams, with circles dedicated to the four phases of the employee journey: join, develop, reward and recognize, and move on. Each circle consists of several employee journey teams, each responsible for a specific process. For example, changing jobs is a journey in the develop phase; earning a bonus or a sabbatical is a rewards journey. (See Figure 3.4.) People Services' objective is to manage as many of the operational aspects of HR as possible, thus freeing HRBPs to focus on strategic priorities. Above all, the most crucial role of People Services is to create differentiated employee experiences that are customized by need and that make ING stand out from its competitors.

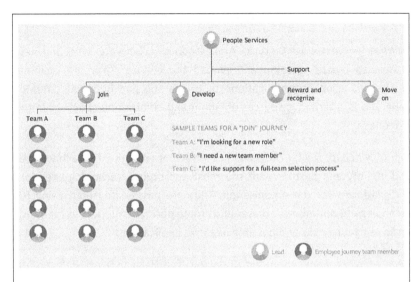

Figure 3.4: ING People Services structure

Communities of Expertise

CoEs create thought leadership, develop the vision, share knowledge, and manage the work portfolio for their particular area of expertise, such as employer branding, workforce planning, or performance management. The expert teams that make up CoEs are divided into two clusters: talent and learning and performance and reward. Working closely with the impact teams, they develop HR processes and products together with their global colleagues (most are developed globally, some locally). The CoEs are also responsible for building HRBPs' capabilities and helping them to work more effectively.[81]

HR capabilities need to change fundamentally

The HR Executive role will change significantly to drive the digital agenda, use advanced analytics and artificial intelligence, leverage organisational and human psychology and innovate for productivity and creativity. The Business Partner, COE and People Service teams will also be made up of new roles and skills sets like Data Scientists, Employee Experience Specialists, Performance Coaches, Bot Monitors, Head of Work Reinvention and Reskilling and the like.

81   Schotkamp & Danoesastro, 2018.

A WEF report called out the following new critical HR roles:[82]

Cultural Ambassador: Cultural Ambassadors collaborate with business leaders to create, develop and embed the culture. They are enablers of change, using communications to bridge the gap between different generations, alternative sources of labour and different perspectives in the workplace.

Digital HR Lead: Digital HR Leads keep track of emerging HR technologies and identify and partner with the most appropriate technology vendors and platforms for the organisation. They are passionate about using HR technology to optimise processes and create positive experiences for talent while mitigating risks and possible negative implications.

Head of Work Reinvention and Reskilling: The Head of Work Reinvention and Reskilling leads the effort to map the skills of the current workforce, reinvent jobs, identify future skills required and optimise how work is done. They champion the view that "no one is left behind" due to technology and automation in the 4IR.

Head of Relevance and Purpose: The Head of Relevance and Purpose looks to continuously align the interests of the organisation with those of its communities and other stakeholders through technology, culture and processes. They work closely with governments, policy-makers and academia to achieve optimal combinations of technology and humans, and ensure the desired impact on society.

Employee Experience Specialist: An Employee Experience Specialist focuses on all the touchpoints in the talent lifecycle, including performance management, reward, benefits and training, through the lens of the employee experience. They are responsible for gathering feedback, analysing it, and championing the employee experience.

Bot Monitor: As chatbots become a more prevalent part of how employees engage with their organisation (questions, applying for jobs, access to policies, collaborating/connecting with colleagues, etc.), there is a growing need for the capability within HR to adopt, manage, monitor and train these bots – which are the most visible and critical element of how the employee experience is increasingly being shaped.

---

82   WEF, 2019.

Chief Learning Officer: While not a new role by any means, as learning moves from being at the fringes of the employee experience to becoming the very heart of it, the Chief Learning Officer becomes a critical and integral part of the leadership team. The Chief Learning Officer uses their knowledge of the adult learning process and passion for lifelong learning to organise and implement upskilling, reskilling and personalised learning. With an enhanced suite of digital tools, they empower people to take ownership of their own careers in the current workforce and beyond.

Head of Insights: The Head of Insights leads the effort to collect valid and valuable insights on human capital. They use data and insights to tell compelling stories, drive decision making through robust measurement and reporting, and identify the quantitative and qualitative business case for human capital investments.

HR Data Scientist: The HR Data Scientist is an expert on people data and systems. They use the vast amount of HR data to analyse employees and their experiences, reduce hiring bias, and identify performance drivers and avenues to better manage the workforce.

Cognizant has an updated view of the new and emerging roles as a result of the COVID-19 pandemic. Some that are relevant to add to the WEF list are:[83]

Work from Home Facilitator: This person will ensure that all remote employees have the technology they need to do their best work. Evaluating, budgeting for and integrating new digital collaboration tools are key responsibilities. Applicants should have a natural fascination with the application of virtual reality (VR) for interaction and collaboration, as VR will be critical to effectively enable remote work.

Head of Business Behaviour: Understanding employee behaviour is a challenging landscape, but it can be made easier by the widespread adoption of sensors and biometric technology in the workplace. Heads of business behaviour will be leaders in workforce intelligence teams, including being responsible for developing data-driven strategies in areas such as employee experience, cross-company collaboration and smart workplace success (which will tackle such issues as how office space impacts the way people work).

---

83   Cognizant, 2020.

Strategic HR Business Continuity Director: This role will protect the workforce and ensure its continued productivity and resilience. The Director will also be a leader in the development, implementation and maintenance of an HR-specific business continuity programme and, in tandem with business continuity planning leads, establish a strategy that enables employees to continue to function without the risk of endangerment. Cross-functional partnership in this role is critical.

Algorithm Bias Auditor: The head of ABA will lead a team that conducts a methodical and rigorous investigation into every algorithm across every business unit within the organisation. The team will work with development teams from tech and business functions for new AI-based applications and will review existing systems. The head of ABA will establish an inventory system that logs and tracks each significant algorithm, its objectives, its input and output, and related human value judgments and consequences.

Second-Act Coach: We believe that the workforce will look very different in the aftermath of the COVID-19 crisis. Despite the need for furloughs and other reshuffling, businesses want to lose as few good employees as possible. The Second-Act Coach will help employees through a four-stage journey: awaken, define, match and prepare. Because many second-acters have just finished up many years of repetitive work, working with them is challenging and rewarding. Defining values and motivators is key to finding the most fitting second act.

Uni4Life Coordinator: The idea here is that more and more employers offer in-house "universities". In a Uni4Life programme, alumni become lifelong learners who enjoy access to specially curated learning opportunities after they graduate. According to Cognizant, Uni4Life AI technology will collect data on lifelong learners to build an up-to-date learning profile. The tool will then use predictive algorithms to make recommendations tied to individual learner profiles and wider labour market data.

Human-Machine Teaming Manager: The future of work will be based on how well companies blend and extend the abilities of humans and machines by making them collaborative. The Human-Machine Teaming Manager will identify tasks, processes, systems and experiences that can be upgraded through newly available technologies and will imagine new approaches, skills, interactions and constructs. This professional will define roles and responsibilities and set the rules for how machines and workers should coordinate to accomplish a task.

Director of Well-Being: The COVID-19 outbreak significantly and immediately increased the requirement that organisations have a well-being strategy in place. Even before the virus, two-thirds of full-time workers experienced burnout on the job. The Director of Well-Being's primary focus is to design, develop and implement well-being programmes aligned with the organisation's culture, mission and values. The vision of the role is a holistic one, with emphasis on weaving mental, emotional, physical and spiritual well-being into the fabric of the organisation.

From these new roles it is clear that critical future skills set for all of HR in the future include:

- digital and data skills;
- agile thinking and risk leveraging;
- interpersonal and communication skills;
- glocalisation skills;
- account and project management;
- customer focus; and
- The Virtual Workplace.[84]

✎ Checklist

1. What operating model do you use as a base for your HR function?
2. Is your HR function future ready?
3. How agile is your HR function?
4. Do you operate like an internal business-focused consultancy with clear projects, deliverables and timelines?
5. Do you have a fluid resourcing model?
6. Are you digitally and analytically strong?
7. Have you created new roles for the new world of work in the HR function?
8. How well respected and influential is your HR function?

---

84   Lee & Yu, 2013.

CHAPTER 4

Design fundamentals for exceptional employee experiences

In this chapter, we learn how to co-develop a differentiated and compelling employee experience using design thinking, employee journey mapping, empathy mapping and analytics. We include the new focus on digital and virtual experiences in the content of this chapter.

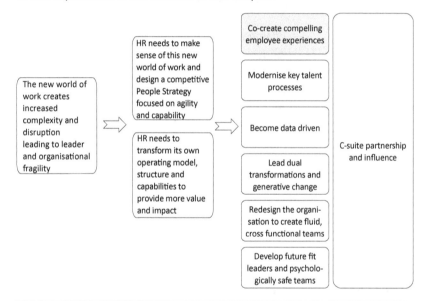

Key ideas

- Pre-COVID, the number one issue on the minds of HR professionals in 2020 was general employee experience; now it is wellness and equity...
- Many organisations have not even started and those that have, are not doing a very good job.
- Employee experience is the whole experience of the employee and is broad in scope and elements – it uses human centred design.

- Employee experience uses employee journeys, design thinking, empathy mapping and analytics.
- Employee experience needs to include the digital experience.
- We need to urgently design for remote employee experiences.
- The employee experience must be measured.

Pre-COVID and social disruption, the number one issue on the minds of HR professionals in 2020 was the general employee experience; now it is wellness and equity

"As the workforce, its fundamental concepts, and its needs evolve, HR too must evolve to become about an all-rounded people experience."[85]

"The best customer experiences bring the company's distinctive brand values and attributes to life, and the same is true of employee experiences. Companies should design them to align with the priorities and differentiators of their brands. For example, if a company wants its brand to be known for automation and speed, then the employees' workplace environment, benefits, performance reviews, and so on should be technology-enabled and fast. If personalization and personal care is what distinguishes a brand, then the employee experience at that company should deliver on those values."[86]

"While HR understands that EX [employee experience] is an important driver in both employee engagement and profitability, only 27% of the C-suite believes the EX will yield a business return. In fact, executives see spending on EX as the least value-adding investment this year, and just one in three (31%) business leaders are accountable for it."[87]

"Companies that exceed their performance goals are 3x more likely to have EX as a core part of their people strategy today, compared to firms not meeting their goals."[88]

---

85 Snowball, 2020.
86 Yohn, 2016.
87 Mercer, 2020b.
88 Mercer, 2020b.

The battle for the hearts and minds of employees is played out daily through their workplace experiences. Gartner[89] defined employee experience (EX) as a worker's perception of their employer from the cumulative effect of their interactions with customers, leaders, teams, processes, policies, tools and work environment. Employee experience bakes employee engagement into each interaction the employee has with the organisation and the people in it. Four critical dimensions of the employee experience are: 1) connection with colleagues and trust in leadership; 2) individual growth and reward opportunities; 3) meaningful work that aligns with employees' values and contributes to a higher purpose; and 4) occurring in an environment that supports productivity and performance.

An early 2020 LinkedIn study of 7,000 HR professionals highlighted the number one issue on the mind of leaders as employee experience.[90] Since then, because of COVID-19, wellness and employee safety has taken over as the key issue to be addressed to become an attractive employer and for an exceptional employee experience. Adding to that is the renewed focus on racial equity, inclusion and belonging as a result of racial tensions and the resulting social response, with many organisations and CEOs taking a firm stand and action on the issue.

Prior to the outbreak, only 5% of non-self-employed US workers worked from home at least half the time. In the space of a few weeks, over half of all US organisations implemented mandatory work from home arrangements for either the whole company or key departments, according to a global pulse survey of companies' COVID responses. Yet given the administrative hurdle of setting up mass remote working at speed, it is understandable that HR's focus on the employee experience may have slipped.[91] Emmett et al.[92] wrote that there is an employee experience moment to be seized as a result of COVID-19. The return phase presents an opportunity for companies to rethink the employee experience in ways that respect individual differences – home lives, skills and capabilities, mindsets, personal characteristics, and other factors – while also adapting to rapidly changing circumstances. Most organisations have done well in addressing immediate safety and stability concerns, but a full return requires organisation-wide commitment to a broader range of needs and to the strongest drivers of work experience, effectiveness, and wellness.

89   Gartner, 2020.
90   Bersin, 2020.
91   Mercer, 2020.
92   Emmett et al., 2020.

Creating a clearly defined and formal employee experience has become a strategic foundation for businesses wanting to flourish in today's global marketplace. Josh Bersin[93] noted that: "EX means that 'we work for the employees' and not the other way around."

Employees have to be treated as humans and as customers, therefore we need to know them, identify moments that matter to them, co-create solutions with them, and pilot, test and scale those solutions using the employee journey as the base and design thinking as the tool. This employee customer design scope is shown in Figure 4.1.

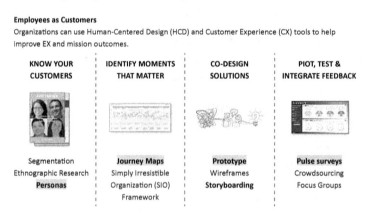

Employees as Customers
Organizations can use Human-Centered Design (HCD) and Customer Experience (CX) tools to help improve EX and mission outcomes.

KNOW YOUR CUSTOMERS	IDENTIFY MOMENTS THAT MATTER	CO-DESIGN SOLUTIONS	PIOT, TEST & INTEGRATE FEEDBACK
Segmentation Ethnographic Research **Personas**	**Journey Maps** Simply Irresistible Organization (SIO) Framework	**Prototype** Wireframes **Storyboarding**	**Pulse surveys** Crowdsourcing Focus Groups

Figure 4.1: Employees as Customers[94]

At the same time, Deloitte[95] reminds us that employees are also different to customers in many ways. First, employees have an enduring, personal relationship with their employers, unlike customers who can stop buying an organisation's products at any time. Second, the employee experience is social; it is built around culture and relationships with others, moving well beyond a focus on an individual employee's needs. Finally, and most relevant to the issue at hand, employees want more than an easy set of transactions – they want a career, purpose and meaning from their work. There are many elements to consider when designing and implementing impactful employee experiences. More work needs to be done on the employee experience-customer service-profit chain to move employee experience up executives' priority list.

---

93   Bersin, 2020.
94   Deloitte, 2017.
95   Deloitte, 2019b.

CASE STUDY: CISCO

The Cisco Global Breakathon gave rise to 105 new HR solutions covering talent acquisition, new hire on-boarding, learning and development, team development, and leadership.

One winning idea focused on the problem of improving the new hire on-boarding process. The winners in this category were actually two ideas: one a mobile app called YouBelong@Cisco to help new hires and their managers navigate the first days and weeks of their new job, and the second, Virtual Concierge, provides a centralised point of support for face-to-face welcoming of a new hire along with digital support. Together they blend the digital and human touch of an employee's first days and weeks at Cisco.[96]

CASE STUDY: IBM

IBM undertook an effort to co-create its EX with employees, bringing employees into the EX design process and iterating EX to ensure the company is meeting their needs.

The company engaged their entire 370,000 workforce in 170 countries through online and face-to-face "innovation jams". For 90 days, two-way communication channels (polls, videos, prototypes etc.) were open for honest discussions and crowdsourcing of ideas. Artificial intelligence also played an important role in running text analytics. The result was the Checkpoint system in which employees set shorter term goals, and managers give at least quarterly feedback on their progress. Goals are set for five dimensions: business results, impact on client success, innovation, collaboration, and skills. When talking about the shift, IBM's CEO Diane Gherson mentioned that IBM employees are "iterating and experimenting", which means that often they are not necessarily working towards what they originally listed as an annual objective, making any longer planning obsolete.

---

96   Meister, 2016.

An on-boarding process that includes ensuring new employees have the tools and information they need, a new Netflix-like digital training and development programme, and a brand-new crowdsourced performance review process, are among the changes the company has implemented.[97]

CASE STUDY: ZOOM

Zoom, a maker of cloud-based video conferencing software, bested all other entries in the category for large employees (500+ workers) and consistently scored an A+ in the areas of work culture, office culture, compensation, perks and benefits, CEO performance and executive team performance.

Efforts to promote gender parity and diversity at Zoom have also pushed the company to the top 5% of large companies that support these cultural initiatives.

The technology group garnered an Employee Net Promoter Score (eNPS) of 94, in which 95% of employees said they would encourage friends to work for the company.[98]

Many organisations have not even started and those that have, are not doing a very good job

First, you need to challenge yourself as to why this has not been done before in your organisation or only done on a very small scale. Several factors make employee experience a challenge today:

- First, many companies have not yet made employee experience a priority for HR leaders, often delegating this problem to an annual engagement survey.

- Second, while some companies have created the C-suite role of Employee Experience Officer, most companies have not assigned

97   Yohn, 2018.
98   Ranosa, 2019.

responsibility to a senior executive or team to design and deliver the employee experience.

- Third, siloed HR departments often find it difficult to obtain the resources needed to address an integrated set of priorities, which range from management practices to the workplace to benefits, and often, the work culture itself.

- Fourth, companies need to update their tools to engage employees on an ongoing basis (with pulse surveys at least) to help HR teams and line leaders understand more fully what the talent they employ expects and values. An employee net promoter score is another important tool in this effort.

- Fifth, many companies remain focused on "point-in-time engagement" and have not yet pulled together the disciplines of performance management, goal setting, diversity, inclusion, wellness, workplace design, and leadership into an integrated framework.[99]

Employee experience is the whole experience of the employee and is broad in scope and elements – it uses human centred design. HR needs to shift from process thinking to experience design thinking with the employee at the centre. An example would be instead of thinking: "What do we need new hires to do on their first day?", HR could think in experience terms, e.g. "What do we want a new employee's first day to be like?"

Employee experience uses employee journeys, design thinking, empathy mapping and analytics

EX starts with understanding and redefining the employee experience journey; it has to be employee -and talent-centric (using tools like empathy maps), collaborative (using design thinking), insightful (powered by best practice and analytics) and engaging (a great and easy user experience).

a. Map the employee experience journey and define the pain points along the journey using employee personas

Employee Experience Journey Mapping is a methodology based upon the very successful Customer Experience Journey Mapping methodology (CXJM).

---

99   Deloitte, 2019b.

Use Employee Experience Journey Mapping to better understand specific employee journeys that may not be generating the outcomes you desire, or you believe you can improve. An employee journey map allows you to put into context the employee experience in a visual format – it is unique to your organisation and demonstrates the values, thoughts and processes of your organisation. It has to be updated regularly to stay relevant.

Along the employee journey of Attract, Select, Onboard, Engage, Retain and Legacy, there needs to be an emotional outcome that matters to the organisation, the candidates and employees. It is important to identify the pain points in the journey. Develop journeys based on the episodes where you've developed insights, breaking down the interactions into both digital and real, with social, mobile and consumer-style experiences for employees.

Oracle developed a very helpful modified Career Journey model that can be used as a base to map the journey as shown in Figure 4.2.

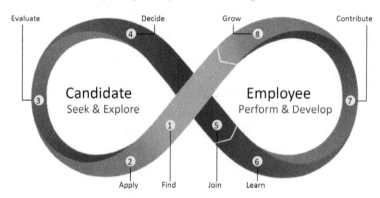

Figure 4.2: Employee Journey Map[100]

No two employees are the same, but you cannot design journeys for each individual, so we use personas. You should define the priority personas in your organisation by segmenting your HR customers, then identify the moments that matter to them, create their journey map and design solutions for them. It is important to look across the different segments to understand the common moments that matter, as that is where early gains can be made.

---

100 Oracle Human Capital Management, 2014.

Employee personas can be created by assessing:

- the age group, education, and tenure of the employee;
- their years of experience;
- their career progression over the years;
- their stated career goals;
- their feedback from employee engagement surveys;
- how often they have switched jobs;
- their performance metrics showing their career development; and
- challenges in the workplace.[101]

BenefitExpress provides ideas for different persona examples in Figure 4.3 below. The personas you choose will be unique to your organisation and industry.

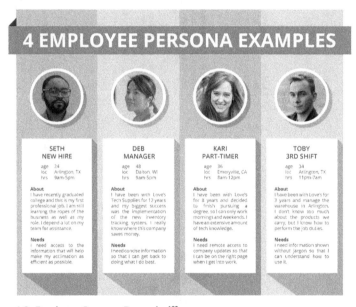

Figure 4.3: Employee Persona Examples[102]

Once you understand the base employee journey and personas, you can map the experiences of the different personas through that journey. These persona-based journey maps becomes the base of an integrated and differentiated employee experience design, as shown in Figure 4.4 below.

101 BasuMallick, 2019.
102 BenefitExpress, 2016

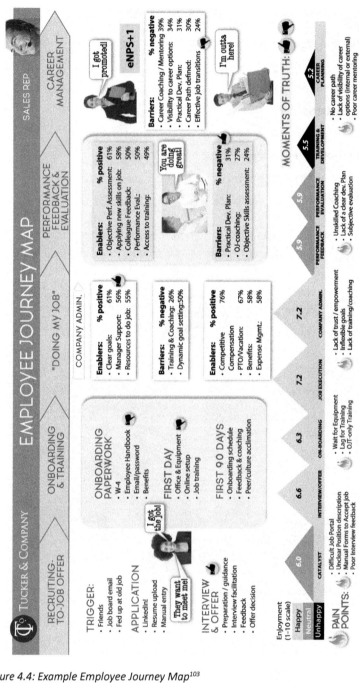

Figure 4.4: Example Employee Journey Map[103]

---

103 Tucker, 2017.

b. Use empathy maps for the different personas to understand their moments that matter, their pain points and their needs across their employee journey

Good design is grounded in a deep understanding of the person for whom you are designing. Designers have many techniques for developing this sort of empathy. An empathy map is one tool to help you synthesise your observations and draw out unexpected insights. Empathy maps help us understand the moments that matter for each employee persona by asking them to complete it with you. Here are the questions you would ask of a representative sample of individuals from the different persona groups about their employee journey:

What does the employee her/himself hear?

- What do co-workers say?

- What does the family say?

- What do friends say?

- What does the boss say?

- What does senior management say?

- What do subordinates say?

Notable differences in language, views expressed, or evaluation may point to a fragmented experience as an employee.

What does the employee say and do?

- What does she say to those around her, along the categories above (co-workers, family, friends, boss, management, her team)?

- Does she do what she says she does? Or are there reasons she doesn't always do what she says she's doing – is it sometimes just a case of "talk the talk" and "walk the walk"?

- Why (not)? And what is behind potential discrepancies? For example, are internal messages and external messages vastly different – and for what reasons? What does it say about the experience that those differences exist?

What does the employee see?

This question relates to the spatial, social and digital environments that influence the employee experience. Office space plays a role but so do behaviours, attitudes, and interactions with people in the workplace. Digital tools and representations are still gaining additional importance, and in general their usability, security, and user experience has become a more important driver of employee experience.

What does the employee think and feel?

What do employees think, based on what they hear, see and say, given their experiences and expectations? How do employees feel based on their experiences and expectations? What is it that makes them feel good, and what is it that causes discomfort?

What are the employee's pains and gains?

Going through the map fields on the left, you will be able to discover themes describing the employee experience and categorise them as pains and gains. Pains and gains serve as starting points to rethink key elements of the employee experience design and prioritise them in terms of effort and impact. Figure 4.5 provides you with a tool to capture your insights.

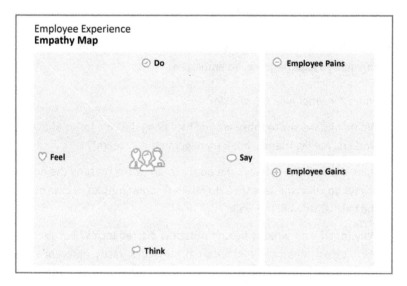

Figure 4.5: Employee experience empathy map[104]

---

104 Managementkits.com, 2019.

c.   Use analytics to supplement and test your empathy map insights

One you have captured your and the employee's perceptions (what they SAY), you want to test it with what they DO. This means triangulating your empathy map insights with employee data and analytics. Traditional employee HR information, semi-structured engagement surveys and unstructured comments from internal and external social platforms can provide insights into potential solutions to experience challenges. Even the Internet of Things can generate useful data about working conditions and personal wellness. Analytics can help you develop insights about specific segments of the population, identify changes in physical and social environments, amplify employee voice, and address issues associated with productivity and tool usage.[105]

Ideate is the mode of your design process in which you aim to generate radical design alternatives to improve or redesign the employee experience. Mentally it represents a process of "going wide" in terms of concepts and outcomes – it is a mode of "flaring" rather than "focus". The goal of ideation is to explore a wide solution space – both a large quantity of ideas and a diversity among those ideas. From this vast depository of ideas you can build prototypes to test with users. The end goal is to synthesise data into interesting findings and create insights which will be useful to you in creating design solutions.

d.   Now start to create new solutions using ideation

Start with some design principles or criteria like desirability, feasibility and viability. Design principles are strategies to solve a design challenge independent of a specific solution. You, as the designer, articulate these principles, translating your findings – such as needs and insights – into design directives. These principles give you a format to capture abstracted, but actionable, guidelines for solutions, and communicate your design intentions to others. The three key guidelines I like to use are Desirability, Feasibility and Viability, as shown in Figure 6. Brainstorm your ideas with questions like: "How might we…", and then test them against the criteria you set.

---

105 IBM Institute for Business Value, 2016.

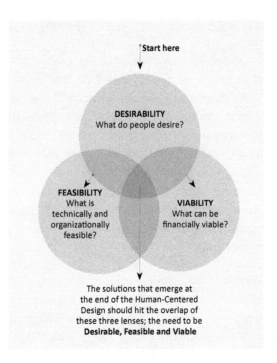

Figure 4.6: Ideation criteria[106]

In order to generate workable ideas for future designs, you can use design sprints. The sprint is a five-day process for answering critical business questions through design, prototyping, and testing ideas with employees.[107] During the design sprint, you will storyboard the new design/new employee experience as shown in Figure 4.7 below.

---

106 Acumen Academy, 2020.
107 Lopushinsky, 2020.

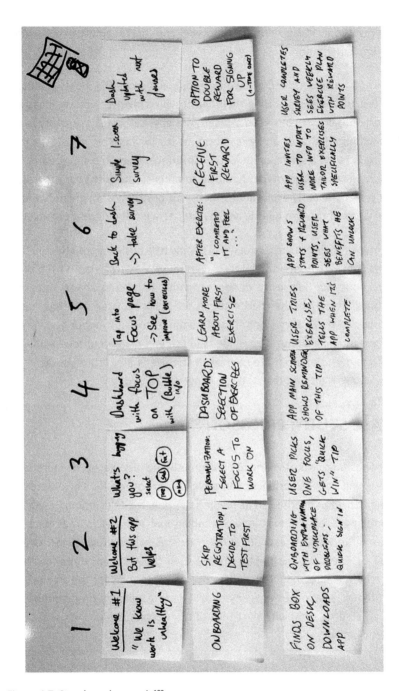

Figure 4.7: Storyboard example[108]

---

108 Höfer, 2017.

e. Test your ideas with a prototype and make adjustments before implementation

Once you have identified a few interesting and workable ideas, prototype and test them before scaling them. Prototyping involves getting ideas and explorations out of your head and into the physical world. A prototype can be anything that takes a physical form, be it a wall of Post-it Notes, a role-playing activity, a space, an object, an interface, or even a storyboard. The resolution of your prototype should be commensurate with your progress in your project. In early explorations keep your prototypes rough and rapid to allow yourself to learn quickly and investigate a lot of different possibilities.

Prototypes are most successful when people (the design team, the user, and others) can experience and interact with them. What you learn from those interactions can help drive deeper empathy, as well as shape successful solutions. Testing is the chance to get feedback on your solutions, refine solutions to make them better, and continue to learn about your users. The test mode is an iterative mode in which you place your low-resolution artefacts in the appropriate context of the user's life. Prototype as if you know you're right, but test as if you know you're wrong.

CASE STUDY: ERICSSON[109]

Emphasising critical moments that matter to people by deliberately designing peak experiences can drive significant results. For example, when Ericsson overhauled its medical offering, the telecommunications company hired a professional comedian and spokesperson to host a 45-minute webcast explaining the new medical coverage plans. Over half of Ericsson's US employees attended the webinar, three-fourths of whom elected healthcare plans that lowered costs for the company. Moreover, employee engagement in voluntary wellness programmes is at an all-time high, with over 75% of the workforce and their spouses participating.

---

109 Mercer, 2020.

Employee experience needs to include the digital experience

With the evolution of the industry has come the emergence of a relatively new term: digital employee experience (DEX). DEX is the sum total of the digital interactions within the work environment. The power of the digital workplace as a lens is that it is very grounded in the day-to-day reality of the digital systems and processes that staff are using.[110]

Digital employee interactions include:

- employees' digital workflows;
- workers' interactions, proficiency, and productivity with their tools and technologies;
- digital adoption of new technology, including onboarding and training; and
- the usability of digital tools.

Australia Post's approach to developing its integrated experience and workforce platform illustrates how an organisation can strive to take a worker-centric view. The organisation began by asking and answering three key questions:

- What do employees require of Australia Post to effectively connect the organisation?
- What must Australia Post enable for employees to feel empowered and motivated to continually evolve and innovate how they do their work?
- What do employees expect to be able to do for themselves in managing both work and personal administrative obligations?

An important part of this step was the creation of eight personas to represent Australia Post's diverse workforce. The resulting understanding of worker needs then informed the project's overall strategy, including the platform's desired future role, its target architecture, an implementation road map, and even a high-level cost estimate. To bring the strategy to life, Australia

---

110 Robertson, 2018.

Post developed creative concepts for its user interface, with a strong focus on user-centred design, enhanced interactivity, clear layout and format, and direct links to important content.[111]

CASE STUDY: UNILEVER

To deliver on strategic growth opportunities, Unilever has worked to release capacity in their workforce while simplifying the existing employee experience. Their research indicated that employees spend a disproportionate amount of time on navigating internal services, losing almost a day of productivity a week on non-value-adding activities, including changing tools, processes and policies. Coupled with the increasing pressure for employers to digitalise the employee environment, Unilever opted for a digital solution to optimise administration and engage employees.

Using an integrated, single point of entry, employees can access information with ease, replacing generic query handling while still customising responses based on employee profiles. Complex queries are resolved using a digital artificial intelligence chatbot through natural language conversation. Unilever complements technology with a front facing People Experience role to support employees end-to-end.

The capacity unlocked through technology and automation is reinvested into human support, which provides employees with a human touch for their day-to-day needs, redirecting focused support where it really matters to the individual. This has resulted in over one million interactions and searches, translating to an estimated 300,000 hours freed up annually for employees and HR. Employee satisfaction scores have increased, and there is a quicker query resolution turnaround time. Employees have more capacity to focus on more productive activities, learning, well-being or finding their purpose.[112]

---

111 Deloitte, 2019.
112 Willis Towers Watson, 2020.

We need to urgently design for remote employee experiences

As employees continue to work from home after the COVID-19 crisis, Employee Experience managers must ensure that their workforce is engaged and progressing forward in their employee journey, says Cameron Smith, Vice President of Product Management and Workforce Engagement Management at Daly City, California-based Genesys. This means not only measuring and assessing employee performance, but looking at whether they are getting sufficient training to perform well and receiving adequate coaching and mentoring from their supervisors. Employee Experience managers will also need to make sure all team members have access to the tools needed to both do their work and constantly improve.

In addition, the Employee Experience manager will be tasked with fostering autonomy among employees. "This involves helping team members feel empowered and encouraging them to self-direct how and when they do their work so they can perform at their peak. This might also involve changing the culture around communication and feedback among employees and their supervisors", said Smith.

Whether it is the first employees back to the office or those who will continue to work remotely for a time, all business functions must collaborate to design systems that are easy, accessible, and available across devices. This means that Employee Experience managers must create a totally seamless digital employee experience that workers can access from anywhere, from onboarding to training to team management. Organisations need to have confidence that people want to do their best for their organisations and their customers, so it is important to take a people-first approach and remember that this inflection point in the world of work will be defined with the employee at the centre and everyone will benefit as a result.

New York City-based WithPulp is a remote-only digital agency. Husam Machlovi, its CEO, says that the new, big focus for Employee Experience managers will be to help remote employees implement their ideal working schedules. Traditional work (9 to 5) had workers online at the same time. The sudden shift to remote work due to COVID-19 has a lot of companies implementing remote work in this way, but remote work will increasingly shift away due to this model.

Remote work will require some time for synchronisation, but for the most part, workers will be able to work on their own schedules. Employee Experience managers will need to advocate on behalf of the employee so that their work life balance is maintained, and they can focus on the results they were brought on board to achieve. Machlovi also believes that the Employee Experience manager's role will evolve to have more ownership of a company's intranet (e.g. a wiki, internal communications, employee directory, onboarding). The intranet will become a more effective way to onboard new employees as well as create communities within a large, remote workforce.[113]

You have to measure the employee experience

"Having in place digital monitoring technologies enables HR teams to have a 360-degree view of the employee experience", says Susan LaMonica, CHRO, Citizen's Financial Group.[114]

Measuring employee experience is in its infancy, however one way is to measure your Employee Net Promoter Score (eNPS). This is a measure of how likely your staff members are to recommend your company as a place to work. It comes from the NPS measure more typically associated with customer satisfaction surveys and it asks employees how likely they are to 'promote' you on a scale from 0 to 10.

According to their answers, they're then classified as 'Promoters', 'Neutral' or 'Detractors'. The eNPS score is then calculated by taking the percentage of detractors and subtracting it from the percentage of promoters to give you an eNPS score from 0-100.

Adidas measures employee experience using a Net Promoter Score with this question: How likely are you to recommend Adidas as a great place to work?" It is a good idea to supplement the eNPS score with other pulse surveys on commitment, satisfaction, job involvement and user experience. An example is shown in Figure 4.8 below.

---

113 Roe, 2020.
114 KPMG, 2019.

How to calculate eNPS:

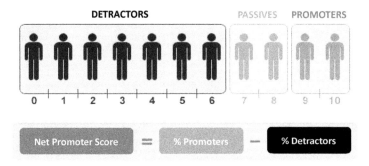

Figure 4.8: Measuring employee engagement efficiently and continuously[115]

✎ Checklist

1. Is employee experience design an HR priority in your organisation?
2. Are you skilled in human centred design?
3. Have you developed employee personas and mapped their employee journeys?
4. What employee listening have you been doing?
5. What data points do you have on your employees' experiences?
6. Have you included the employee digital experience in the consideration of the employee experience?
7. How have you adapted your employee experiences for the new way of working virtually?
8. Are you working closely with Marketing and IT to design employee experiences?

---

115 Netigate, 2020.

CHAPTER 5

Modernise key talent processes

In this chapter, we examine the changes in talent management in the new world of work and the processes that most frustrate managers – talent acquisition and onboarding, performance management, and learning and development. We also highlight the increased importance of employee well-being, equity and inclusion as an integral part of the talent management process.

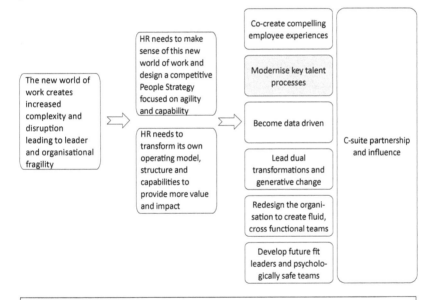

Key ideas

- A new decade brings a new talent direction.
- Talent looks completely different in the new world of work – use Talent Portfolio Management.
- Managers are frustrated with the time it takes to hire talent and the quality of the talent – fix the process, the candidate experience and the employment brand.
- Managers and employees hate the performance management process – fix it.

> - Significant skill disruption changes the way in which organisational learning and development are viewed and operationalised.
> - It is urgent to turn in-person leadership programmes into effective virtual learning to enable virtual working, engagement and performance.
> - Well-being has become critical to organisational sustainability.
> - Diversity, Equity and Inclusion is becoming a key talent and culture attractor.

A new decade brings a new talent direction

"As we live through the resulting turmoil and we are tested in terms of both business continuity and the world's capacity to formulate a global response, it is clear we need to focus at once on the near and long term. We must stop and ask: Is today's approach to work and workforce transformation sustainable? Will our work models attract new generations? How will we reinvigorate our businesses? How can we ensure our employee value proposition meets rising health, wealth and career concerns? And are existing practices agile enough to withstand this and future unpredictable events' impact on profit?"[116]

"Agility starts with knowing your talent ecosystem – that is, knowing who you have and where. Two in five HR leaders acknowledge they don't know what skills they have in their workforce. And only one in three are quantifying the skills gap against business objectives, which over half of HR leaders say is a challenge, up 20% from last year."[117]

The *Mercer 2020 Talent Report* shows the different ways in which executives are rethinking their approach to the future of their organisations. They are swiftly adopting future of work strategies to compete and stay relevant, while preparing to face a very likely economic downturn. If macroeconomic conditions continue to trend unfavourably, companies plan to double down on strategic partnerships (40%), use more variable talent pools (39%) and invest in automation (34%). These strategies will speed up the changes

---

116 Mercer, 2020.
117 Mercer, 2020.

we're seeing in how we trade goods and services, operate our businesses and connect with one another.

Talent looks completely different in the new world of work – use Talent Portfolio Management

"Every talent management process in use today was developed half a century ago. It's time for a new model."[118]

"2 in 5 HR leaders say they do not know what skills they have in their workforce today".[119]

"Despite feeling stalled at certain career levels, over half of employees trust their employer to prepare them for the future of work (61%), help them plan for retirement (58%) and provide a new role if their job significantly changes (57%)."[120]

"77% of Executives believe freelance and gig workers will substantially replace full-time employees within the next 5 years."[121]

The classical employment model of hiring permanent employees to manage work activities is breaking down as employee preferences change and organisations tap into capabilities beyond traditional boundaries. Talent communities and social media are making it easy for talent to connect with employers even before the opportunity for employment arises, as well as stay in touch after completing an engagement. The increased mobility of employees, as well as a rise in the number of contingent and project-based assignments, means that talent may come and go in a company multiple times during their careers.[122]

New ways of thinking about – and managing – talent are desperately needed to compete in the digital and virtual era. Organisations need to shift from

---

118 Cappelli, 2008.
119 Mercer, 2020.
120 Mercer, 2020.
121 Mercer, 2020.
122 Mercer, 2015.

Talent Management to Talent Portfolio Management. Hallenbeck et al.[123] defined Talent Portfolio Management as: "The organizational capability and mindset of accomplishing work through a portfolio of talent enabled by agile talent processes." They called out three types of talent that make up a Talent Portfolio: traditional, gig and technology-driven talent, as per Figure 5.1. The first prong is traditional talent, i.e. your current full-time and part-time workforce, which likely makes up the bulk of your existing portfolio. The second prong is gig economy talent, including freelance talent locally and globally. The third is technology-driven talent, including robotics and artificial intelligence. Together they comprise the capabilities needed to collectively deliver organisational outcomes.

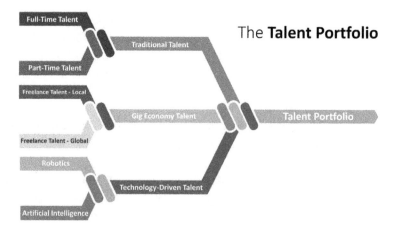

Figure 5.1: The Talent Portfolio[124]

Developing a talent ecosystem for key capabilities will be important to remain competitive in an environment of continuous disruption and cost pressure. Technological advances are making this type of collaboration and external partnering more feasible. Project teams spanning organisational and geographical boundaries, which include representatives from supplier companies, customer organisations and independent contracting third parties, can now rely on shared databases, cloud platforms, teleconferencing and other collaborative software.

---

123 Hallenbeck et al., 2018.
124 Hallenbeck et al., 2018.

Today, the sources of where to find properly skilled talent are dynamic. These sources certainly don't stop and end at corporate walls, and some companies are placing big bets on contingent work of all types – gig, variable staffing, independent contractors and more. HR still finds hiring externally to fill skill gaps the most effective strategy (60%), however 65% of HR leaders say that even if they raise salaries, they will not be able to find the right talent due to talent shortages. It is no surprise , therefore, that 76% of companies are planning to build from within this year.[125]

CASE STUDY: PROCTOR & GAMBLE

Proctor & Gamble's (P&G) R&D team was asked to develop a strategy for leveraging global scientists, suppliers, and networks for half of their future innovations. The idea was not to replace but rather to extend the reach, productivity, and capability of P&G's 7,500 product development specialists and researchers by connecting them, using both propriety and open networks, with suppliers (and their 50,000 R&D specialists) and scientists around the world.

P&G's Connect and Develop network uses multiple talent approaches, including:

- hiring retired R&D scientists for specific projects (a form of freelance talent);

- conducting competitions for technical and product development challenges, providing awards for specific challenges using proprietary and third-party open source markets such as InnoCentive; and

- deepening relationships with its supplier network to identify solutions to product development challenges (a form of partnership talent that involves licensing and purchasing product ideas and technologies).[126]

---

125 Mercer, 2020.
126 Mercer, 2015.

TOOLS: PWC'S SKILLS EXPANDER AND FAETHM

There are great digital and AI tools available on the market to help tackle the challenge of job transformation and upskilling.

SKILLS EXPANDER

PWC have launched Skills Expander, a workforce development digital platform that supports businesses across their entire reskilling value chain. Powered by a highly sophisticated data analytics engine, Skills Expander helps to integrate the workforce development process from job matching to assessment and skills training. It can help with workforce planning, skills assessment, and skills and training matching.

Through its data analytics capabilities, the Skills Expander digests various job descriptions and CVs, breaking them down to create an inventory of currently available skills and new skills required. The tool does not just base itself on keyword search matching; instead, it infers meaning and also draws information from the existing skill frameworks of the organisation, sector or a specific industry best-practice, before contextualising results to the reality of the local job market.[127]

FAETHM

Faethm is a fast-growth and globally unique AI Analytics SaaS Platform. Launched in Sydney in late 2017, Faethm is already helping companies and governments in North America, Europe and Asia Pacific to create economic and social value from the impact of emerging technologies.

Faethm's platform blends proprietary analytics with client data to predict the impact of emerging technology on any job, workforce, company, industry, location or economy. As a result, this enables companies and governments to:

---

127 Schouten & Munshi, 2020.

- validate and prioritise digital transformation agendas;

- re-skill employees for the future;

- develop better strategies and policies; and,

- make smarter investment decisions.[128]

Managers are frustrated with the time it takes to hire talent and the quality of the talent – fix the process, the candidate experience and the employment brand

Talent attraction, more important than ever in tight labour markets, hinges not only on the employee brand, but on the culture of the organisation and whether employees feel they can grow and shape the trajectory of the business. Many managers are still frustrated with the amount of time the process takes and their inability to source and recruit the best talent with the right future capabilities. The definition of talent acquisition spans employer branding; recruitment marketing; the process of recruitment itself, which includes candidate relationship management, an onboarding plan that involves succession planning and talent development; and continuous strategic alignment with C-level goals.

The candidate experience is increasingly pivotal to job seekers and potential employees considering a role within an organisation. Once an afterthought, this journey is now regarded as a crucial element of an employer's brand strategy. Each step along the candidate's journey should be authentic, reinforce the employer's culture and provide transparency into how employees are valued within an organisation. Using design thinking, the candidate experience needs to start with the definition of the candidate journey to identify pain points and moments that matter. It culminates in the design of an engaging and user-friendly career site, compelling and inclusive job postings, and the use of candidate experience surveys. Pre-engagement is critical to the process. Organisations that set expectations about the process, provide interview tips and continuously communicate with candidates see positive outcomes.

---

128 Faethm.ai, 2020.

The onboarding journey has to match the candidate experience. Airbnb schedules different lunches and meetings before people join to understand their colleagues and the workplace better. Aurecon, meanwhile, built an engaging online visual and personalised employment contract experience for new employees. A memorable first day, a buddy, a small gift, a functioning laptop and an access pass makes the transition so much better. Intentional immersions covering the culture, introductions to all stakeholders and an understanding of strategies, goals and early development opportunities all help with acclimatising. Celebrations of milestones should also be continuous.

CASE STUDY: INFINEON[129]

It is hard to imagine the modern world without the semiconductor; from smartphones to solar cells, cars and communications infrastructure, semiconductors help power everyday life. The challenge for the global semiconductor company, Infineon, was to come up with the best possible solutions to serve its markets, for which it needed to attract the best talent possible.

Five years ago, the company hired around 300 mainly IT and digital talent each year – not nearly enough to grow their market position. HR, in conjunction with Infineon's strategy department, identified the 12 most critical – but hard to fill – roles required by the business, such as software engineers, field application engineers and product marketing specialists.

Infineon hypothesised how the recruitment process could be optimised in a competitive market for these positions. The firm realised it could capitalise on its own, as yet untapped, evidence; they delved into their talent analytics to understand the needs, profile and preferences of previously successful hires.

---

129 Mercer, 2020.

Armed with these insights, the talent acquisition team designed a hypothetical candidate profile (or persona) for each of the 12 critical roles, taking into account the tasks, competencies and personality types uncovered by the data. From this, the HR team was able to identify the attraction drivers for different personas.

The company realised that combining the data-driven persona work with human intuition would be the key to success. The latter involved deploying a design thinking approach to create targeted messages, marketing and sourcing activities to attract candidates. Given the scarcity of candidates in the market, the company zeroed in on efforts to cultivate human relationships such as personalised newsletters, using a sales-like CRM system, alumni management, and redefining hiring managers' and recruiters' role to one of selling the company.

There has been a significant positive benefit for the business. The data-driven, human-augmented approach reduced headhunter costs by 80%, while hiring has increased fivefold. Today Infineon hires more than 1,500 people a year.

CASE STUDY: BUPA

BUPA worked to build an influential Employment Brand Strategy by personalising their purpose and using messages that make a connection between the broader purpose and the candidates' personal role in furthering that purpose. They mapped critical episodes (encounters) across processes and channels of talent acquisition and selected encounters that had the most potential for developing deeper meanings and human connections. They then immersed themselves in the candidate experience and defined a desired candidate experience based on what they wanted the candidate to think, feel and do.[130]

---

130 Corzo, 2016.

CASE STUDY: AURECON

The global engineering and infrastructure advisory company, Aurecon, uses a visual employment contract, eliminating more than 4,000 words from their employment contracts to create a succinct and meaningful visual contract that uses illustrations to complement the text.

Developed in partnership with Camilla Andersen, a Law Professor at the University of Western Australia, Aurecon's employment contracts are legally binding contracts in which Aurecon and its employees are represented by characters – free of legal jargon and akin to a comic strip format. (See Figures 5.2 and 5.3 below.)

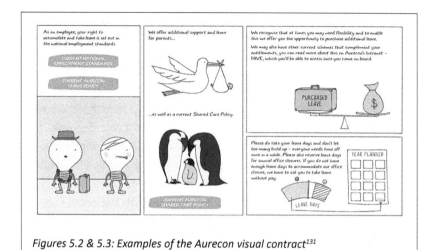

Figures 5.2 & 5.3: Examples of the Aurecon visual contract[131]

Managers and employees hate the performance management process – fix it!

"The worst-kept secret in companies has long been the fact that the yearly ritual of evaluating (and sometimes rating and ranking) the performance of employees epitomizes the absurdities of corporate life."[132]

"Leaders can build resilience and agility by rethinking their approach to performance management in the wake of the COVID-19 pandemic."[133]

Even if you have given the candidate a great recruitment and onboarding experience, the performance management process can disengage them. Most corporate performance-management systems don't work today because they are rooted in models for specialising and continually optimising discrete work tasks. These models date back more than a century, to Frederick W. Taylor. When businesses adopted agile methods in their core operations, they dropped the charade of trying to plan a year or more in advance how projects would go and when they would end. In many cases, the first traditional HR practice to go was the annual performance review, along with employee goals that "cascaded" down from business and unit objectives each year. As individuals worked on shorter term projects of

---

131 Aurecon, 2018.
132 Ewenstein, Hancock & Komm, 2016.
133 Heidrick & Struggles, 2020.

various lengths, often run by different leaders and organised around teams, the notion that performance feedback would come once a year, from one boss, made little sense; they needed more of it, more often, from more people.[134]

Many companies, such as GE, the Gap and Adobe Systems have dropped ratings, rankings, and annual reviews, practices that GE, for one, had developed into a fine art in previous decades. What these companies want to build – objectives that are more fluid and changeable than annual goals, frequent feedback discussions rather than annual or semi-annual ones, forward-looking coaching for development rather than backward-focused rating and ranking, a greater emphasis on teams than on individuals – looks like the exact opposite of what they are abandoning.

Good data are crucial to the new processes, not least because so many employees think that the current evaluation processes are full of subjectivity. Zalando, a leading European e-retailer, is currently implementing a real-time tool that crowdsources both structured and unstructured performance feedback from meetings, problem-solving sessions, completed projects, launches and campaigns. Employees can request feedback from supervisors, colleagues and internal "customers" through a real-time online app that lets people provide both positive and more critical comments about each other in a playful and engaging way. Relatively easy and inexpensive to build (or to buy and customise), such performance-development applications are promising – but challenging.

COVID-19 and recent social pressures have accelerated the challenges we face with performance management. In the current environment, the process has to shift even more to being less formal and more fluid. Time-consuming and often demotivating, performance reviews can put the focus on completing the process rather than on actually improving performance. Even more, they assume a level playing field for all employees, which is often not the case. For example, employees from underrepresented groups including racial and ethnic minorities, women, and people from disadvantaged socioeconomic backgrounds may be held to a different set of standards. And more recently, home-schooling responsibilities during the pandemic have added considerable productivity challenges for working parents of young children. Going forward, organisations should focus on showing empathy and fairness to help people

---

134 Cappelli & Tavis, 2018.

perform at their best. In part because the pandemic has had a negative impact on pay and bonuses, many leaders are finding opportunities to experiment with approaches that decouple performance discussions from other parts of the talent management process. The crisis has already prompted many organisations to review their objectives. In order to reduce anxiety and provide focus in the short term, for example, many are revisiting long term output objectives and increasing the frequency with which these objectives are reviewed and updated.[135]

CASE STUDY: ADOBE

In 2012, Adobe's People Resources leaders decided that annual performance reviews were too time consuming, negative and slow to be the foundation for performance management moving forward. Through an unplanned conversation with an Indian journalist, events were set into motion rapidly and the company announced the end to annual performance reviews a few months later. The "Check-in" – a two-way, ongoing dialogue between managers and employees – became the new standard at Adobe, resulting in dramatic efficiency gains, more effective performance management and higher employee engagement and retention. It includes:

- setting written expectations at the start of the year, which are revisited regularly. The company suggests quarterly meetings at a minimum. A goal-setting form is provided for employees who would like to use it, but no set format is required;

- providing ongoing feedback focused on performance throughout the year, and ideally as real-time as possible so the right behaviours can be reinforced;

- eliminating all mandates around timing, methods and written reviews; and

- providing a budget for salary raises and equity grants, which happen once annually in the Rewards Check-in, so people managers and senior leaders can adjust awards based on their best judgment. There are no ratings, rankings or prescribed awards required.[136]

---

135 Heidrick & Struggles, 2020.
136 Morris, 2016.

CASE STUDY: JOHNSON & JOHNSON

Johnson & Johnson offered its businesses the chance to participate in an experiment; they could try out a new continual-feedback process, using a customised app with which employees, peers, and bosses could exchange comments in real-time.

The new process was an attempt to move away from J&J's event-driven "five conversations" framework (which focused on goal setting, career discussion, a midyear performance review, a year-end appraisal, and a compensation review) and toward a model of ongoing dialogue. Those who tried it were asked to share how well everything worked, what the bugs were, and so on. The experiment lasted three months, with only 20% of the managers in the pilot actively participating initially.

The inertia from prior years of annual appraisals was hard to overcome, but then the company used training to show managers what good feedback could look like and designated "change champions" to model the desired behaviours on their teams. By the end of the three months, 46% of managers in the pilot group had joined in, exchanging 3,000 pieces of feedback.[137]

Significant skill disruption changes the way in which organisational learning and development are viewed and operationalised

"One in three employees believe their job will not exist in a few years due to AI and automation."[138]

"The emergence of new skills and the requirement to learn, unlearn and relearn skills faster and more frequently is a top concern for organizations and governments. The workforce now rates the opportunity to learn among the top reasons for taking a job. Changes in technology, longevity, work practices and business models have created a tremendous demand for continuous, lifelong development. As learning moves from the fringes to

---

137 Cappelli & Travis, 2018.
138 Mercer, 2020.

the centre of the talent experience, leading organizations are taking steps to deliver learning to their people in a more personal way, integrating work and learning more tightly with each other."[139]

"Chief Learning Officers from leading global companies that we surveyed say that they have stopped and/or postponed the delivery of in-person leadership programs due to Covid-19. Health concerns, travel and cost restrictions have been cited as the key reasons for the decline in the number of leaders who will attend in-person leadership programs over the coming 12 months."[140]

Since the pandemic, 59% of UK Learning and Development (L&D) professionals say they have started to develop a stronger learning culture within their businesses[141], while LinkedIn Learning noted a 60% increase in C-level executives taking learning courses in March and April, compared to January and February.[142]

With transformation being an everyday reality, reskilling is the biggest opportunity and challenge of the decade. Without accelerating our progress on the skills agenda, we won't have the talent to take advantage of the new jobs we're creating. This is both a business and an HR challenge, and it therefore demands organisation- wide interventions to deliver results. Companies that unlock reskilling at speed and scale will transform at a pace that leaves their competitors behind.[143]

Globally, reskilling is seen as the top talent activity most capable of delivering a return on investment (ROI) in the eyes of executives. And this ROI assumption makes sense, given that 99% of all companies are both embarking on a transformation this year and reporting significant skill gaps. Combined with executives' increasing apprehension around talent migration this year (up from 4% in 2017 to 38% in 2020), skill supply concerns are high on the priority list. When asked what helps them thrive, employees' number one response is recognition for their contributions, alongside opportunities to learn new skills and technologies (43% and 42%, respectively). Only two in

139 WEF, 2019
140 Van Dam & Coates, 2020.
141 Murlidhar, 2020.
142 Murlidhar, 2020.
143 Mercer, 2020.

five CEOs are held accountable for employee reskilling, however, compared to almost three-quarters of CHROs. Without the business taking shared responsibility for identifying future skills needed and the pathway forward, HR will struggle to have the impact required.[144]

Now is the time for companies to be forward thinking, to anticipate which roles will be needed tomorrow to deliver on future customer needs, and to identify where the skills gaps are in order to fill them. Leaders have the task of solving the complex process of building core competence, as well as continuously developing emerging skill sets required for companies to thrive in this constantly disrupted environment. Speed has also become a critical factor of success, and the pressure is on to ensure faster and more agile delivery, just in time development, and on the job learning opportunities. In addition, corporate learning needs to adopt digital standards and leverage technology and culture to provide a more engaging, personalised, interactive, tailor-made, and ultimately more impactful, learner experience (EFMD, 2018). McGowan (2019) called learning the "new pension". The appreciation for the value of learning from leaders and employees alike will help cement its position as a strategic business priority.

But right now, we are not delivering the required impact. In a 2019 *Harvard Business Review* article, Glaveski[145] wrote that 75% of 1,500 managers surveyed from across 50 organisations were dissatisfied with their company's L&D function; 70% of employees reported that they did not have mastery of the skills needed to do their jobs; only 12% of employees applied new skills learnt in L&D programmes to their jobs; and only 25% of respondents to a McKinsey survey believed that training measurably improved performance. Glaveski attributed this to learning taking place at the wrong time, as well as people learning the wrong things and quickly forgetting what they had learnt. In fact, Deloitte found that the Net-Promoter Score of L&D rated by non-HR professionals was -8.[146]

Most companies focus on upgrading skills for near term advantage, such as improving digital literacy in areas such as marketing and IT. But these efforts often distract from the reskilling agenda, which can address system-wide needs to fill new and emerging roles with reskilled talent from within a

---

144 Mercer, 2020.
145 Glaveski, 2019.
146 Deloitte, 2014.

company's own ecosystem. The focus on reskilling also opens up alternative career options for those at risk of displacement and builds movement into the talent system.[147]

Companies that transform their learning and development organisations are therefore not only able to accelerate skills development, but can also dramatically improve employee engagement and retention. But what skills should organisations focus on? Ashoka and McKinsey & Co[148] defined the required future skills as a combination of digital, and human skills, while a WEF report[149] described how learning needs to change in organisations to be relevant to 4IR.

Amazon recently pledged $700 million to retrain 100,000 employees for higher-skilled jobs in technology (for example, training warehouse employees to become basic data analysts), while JPMorgan Chase made a five-year, $350 million commitment to develop technical skills in high demand – in part targeting its own workers. And Walmart has already invested more than $2 billion in wages and training programmes, including Walmart Pathways, which educates entry-level employees about the company's business model and helps workers develop valuable soft skills.

One European bank made a huge investment in digital learning as an alternative to laying off thousands of staff in the wake of the digitisation of its core business. It has not only introduced a learning team with video-production specialists, graphic designers, and illustrators, but also developed a highly sophisticated mobile app. The quality is so good that the learning-and-development unit has turned itself into a revenue centre by selling the app to other companies. That money comes in addition to savings from the elimination of some in-person learning sessions, which generated travel expenses and required time away from work. Many employees report that they spend up to half of their time on the app outside working hours, on top of learning modules during the day. Over several years, the bank has involved more than 10,000 employees in the programme, and has subsequently placed many in new lines of business (Hancock et al., 2020). Reskilling and upskilling will need to continue over longer, multiple and diverse careers. We are moving from I and T shaped discipline identity to transdisciplinary X

---

147 Mercer, 2020.
148 McKinsey & Co, 2018.
149 WEF, 2019.

shaped thinking, where humans and machines collaborate from discipline-agnostic perspectives to find and frame complex challenges.[150]

Doig[151] described these identities in more detail. The I-shaped learner has depth in one (or several) area(s) of knowledge or skillsets, often referred to as stocks of knowledge. There are many industries and professions where deep expertise is critical, but in an increasingly complex world, knowledge does not stand as a unique discipline without reference to others. Those who simply keep their heads down in their own silos of expertise are less desirable for employers if they cannot relate to others. Morton T. Hansen referred to these as 'lone stars' who do their own work well but do not contribute beyond that. The T-shaped learner was popularised by the CEO of IDEO, Tim Brown. This learner/worker has a broad range of skills in selected niches, but along with this has deep expertise in the ability to work with others. In a T-shaped learner, the vertical stroke still refers to deep knowledge or the skills of an I-shaped learner, but the horizontal stroke adds the ability to collaborate across disciplines. The horizontal stroke adds breadth to a learner and connects more to the world of multidisciplinary thinking. Based on his research on collaboration, Hansen suggested that T-shaped managers are the way of the future as they are able to perform their individual work well (the vertical), while also contributing effectively across the whole organisation (the horizontal). Whether in managers, workers or learners, the key is both strong expertise and the ability to connect.

The X-shaped learner moves in the transdisciplinary space, where learning includes interdisciplinarity with a participatory approach and a more holistic focus on a common goal. Learning in this space often focuses on a problem of society at large, such as climate change and global warming. Heather McGowan referred to this space as leading to the end of occupation identity, i.e. where it becomes less about knowledge and skills at a particular point and time or a 'one-occupation self', and more about finding purpose. An X-shaped learner has a higher degree of self-awareness, adaptive capacity and the competencies to thrive in the future. These uniquely human skills are grounded in empathy and purpose. X-shaped learning moves from stocks of knowledge to requiring us to be in the state of learning flow, continually adapting to the environment.

---

150 McGowan & Shipley, 2019.
151 Doig, 2019.

The types of skills humans need are changing significantly. These requirements necessitate upskilling and reskilling at scale. Upskilling means that we add digital skills for an old job, while reskilling means acquiring completely different skills for a digital/data job. Furthermore, we need human reskilling for jobs where human interaction and relationships are becoming more critical – usually in direct contact with customers. Finally, meta skilling refers to the generic skills that all employees need to thrive in the new world of work, including skills such as adaptability, self-direction, resilience and a growth mindset. Human, digital and meta skills have to be prioritised in ongoing, always available, real-time learning journeys. These skills are shown in Figure 5.4.

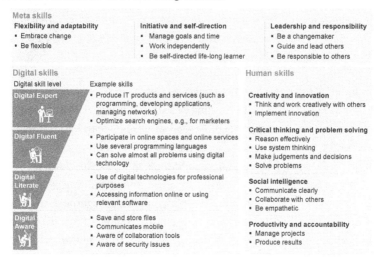

Figure 5.4: Meta, digital and human skills for the 21st century[152]

Reskilling and upskilling training cannot be delivered in traditional ways. Established L&D programmes consisted of several days of classroom learning with no follow-up sessions, even though people tend to forget what they have learnt without regular reinforcement. Today's learners are resistant to learning that is removed from the here and now and that is delayed. Learners need to learn rapidly, adapt, collaborate and be self-directed. We need to bridge the time gap between what is learnt and when people are called on to apply that learning (retention and transfer). We cannot retain

152 Askoka & McKinsey, 2018.

the vast amount of information we need to apply in our work, and therefore need access to that information at the time of need. Learners are also short on time and attention – according to Deloitte, they only have about 24 minutes available for learning a week.[153]

Dani Johnson[154] urged L&D practitioners to move from the 70-20-10 model that is 30 years old and lacking in supporting evidence, to continuous learning models. She defined continuous learning as "structuring resources, expectations, and learning culture in such a way as to encourage employees to learn continuously throughout their tenure with the organization". The L&D function includes designing learning journeys – continuous learning opportunities that take place over a period of time and include L&D interventions such as fieldwork, pre- and post-classroom digital learning, social learning, on-the-job coaching and mentoring, and short workshops. The main objectives of a learning journey are to help people develop the required new competencies in the most effective and efficient way, and to support the transfer of learning to the job.[155]

The learning design process is changing significantly to become a human centred design process, with learning designers working with data scientists. Data are the foundation of digital-age learning; as learning moments are captured, they generate a data footprint which can be analysed to understand a person's learning history. But beyond looking at past performance, data can also be fed back to the learner to boost engagement as well as make future learning more personalised. This ability and eagerness to visualise and communicate data, and allow them to shape future behaviour, is typical of a data scientist, and distinguishes them from a mere data analyst. Equally, defining the right problem to solve is essential. Approaching this task as a design thinker implies doing two things. First, observation takes centre stage; rather than relying on what one says, observation can help discern what people really need. Second, constant questioning is essential; only after multiple rounds of questioning are the true issues revealed. This discipline allows a design thinker to suspend judgment and look at the problem through the customer's eyes – an empathy that differentiates his or her approach from more deductive approaches to problem definition.

---

153 Deloitte, 2017.
154 Johnson, 2014.
155 Johnson, 2014.

EFMD[156] wrote that "Digital Age Learning is a more profound transformation of the learning process, using digital tools to re-think what needs to be done and exploiting entirely new opportunities that are presented. For instance, using algorithms to personalise the learning experience. Digitalisation is a process of rethinking what is possible and moving learning onto a different level of use and complexity". Technology can transform one- or two-days of upskilling into a continuous development journey; touchpoints, for example, between facilitators and delegates can be increased, progress can be regularly assessed, and continuous, personalised feedback provided. Furthermore, resource material can be made available anytime, anywhere, with course content easily updated as the business' context and strategy shifts. Tools like HowNow, Learnerbly, edX and General Assembly bring learning opportunities into the workplace.

COVID-19 introduced a new challenge to the L&D teams – that of turning in-person programmes into highly effective virtual learning. Converting in-person programmes is not about just digitising an existing in-person programme; it is about the art and science of effective virtual design. There are five guiding principles to consider in this regard:

1. Design for user experience, i.e. easy access, usage and navigation; personalisation; interaction with peers and faculty; an engaging and motivating experience; sufficient breaks; group sizes that support learning outcomes; skilled faculty; and linked to relevant and real-world outcomes.

2. Use evidence-based pedagogy and instructional strategies. Consider the cognitive load of the programme, space out learning, repeat content and include assignments and exercises.

3. Enable pedagogy through learning technology. Provide a seamless experience, use chat functions, use polls, create breakout rooms, use emoticon buttons, leverage whiteboards, enable screen sharing, invite participation, use quizzes and use video and animation.

4. Advance learning through AI, data and analytics. Use the data gathered during the learning to improve in real-time and evolve the design and delivery to increase effectiveness and impact.

---

156 EFMD, 2018.

5. Develop your facilitators and faculty for virtual delivery excellence. Facilitating virtually requires a unique skillset and online teaching style.[157]

CASE STUDY: AT&T

With its industry moving from cables and hardware to the internet and the cloud, AT&T is in a sprint to reinvent itself. AT&T employs about 280,000 people, most of whom got their education and foundational job training in a different era. The average tenure at the company is 12 - 22 years if you don't count people working in call centres. But rather than hiring new talent wholesale, AT&T has chosen to rapidly retrain its current employees while striving to engender a culture of perpetual learning.

The first task of AT&T's programme – dubbed Workforce 2020 (or WF2020) – was to identify the skills the firm would need and create a blueprint for sourcing them internally. Managers documented existing gaps and formulated "future role profiles" for themselves and their teams. Every manager in AT&T's network and technology strategy organisation, which constitutes roughly half the firm's professional workforce, was assigned a new role and expected to get the training or credentials to fill it. WF2020 consolidated 250 roles across the company into 80. The goal was to radically simplify and standardise role structures, in order to increase job mobility and foster the development of interchangeable skills.[158]

CASE STUDY: NESTLÉ

Nestlé recently completed a review of how learning could play a more strategic role in a world dominated by the need for innovation, agility, and social, mobile and digital technology. The company's CLO, Fausto Palumbo, presented a bold view that learning could be a strategic lever within the organisation to change the way employees think and act. This led to a review of enterprise-wide leadership programmes and the initiation of a pilot programme with the mission of reimagining the learning experience for senior executives.

---

157 van Dam & Coates, 2020.
158 HBR, 2016.

Instead of a lecture-based programme, Nestlé developed a multifaceted experiential learning model that included a wide variety of activities:

- A multi-day, high-stress simulation around key leadership topics.

- Reactions to real-time/simulated data from product-specific social and mobile feeds.

- Product development by widely distributed design and development teams using digital technologies.

- Prototype development of new products using digital printing.

To ensure that learning was not an isolated event but rather integrated into daily work, the company set up a series of video and digital presentations before the live learning module was launched, and also built follow-up events.[159]

CASE STUDY: IBM

People consume content on their phones and tablets now – they use YouTube and TED talks to get up to speed on things they don't know. So we had to put aside our traditional learning-management system and think differently about education and development. Again, we brought in our Millennials, brought in our users, and codesigned a learning platform that is individually personalized for every one of our 380,000 IBMers.

It's tailored by role, with intelligent recommendations that are continually updated. And it's organized sort of like Netflix, with different channels. You can see how others have rated the various offerings. There's also a live-chat adviser, who helps learners in the moment.

With Watson Analytics, we're able to infer people's expertise from their digital footprint inside the company, and we compare that with where they should be in their particular job family. The system is cognitive, so it knows you – it has ingested the data about your skills and is able to give you personalized learning recommendations.[160]

159 Haims, Stempel & van der Vyver, 2015.
160 Burrell, 2018.

Well-being has become critical to organisational sustainability

"As the line between work and life blurs, providing a robust suite of well-being programs focused on physical, mental, financial, and spiritual health is becoming a corporate responsibility and a strategy to drive employee productivity, engagement, and retention. While organizations are investing heavily in this area, our research reveals there is often a significant gap between what companies are offering and what employees value and expect."[161]

"One in three employees say economics 'mostly' or 'entirely' drives decisions at their organization. Nearly two in three (63%) employees feel at risk of burnout this year. The primary reasons are a lack of rewards for effort given (30%), followed by workload (29%). Despite health and well-being ranked as executives' number one concern this year only one in five have targets related to achieving this outcome. A study by Stanford Business Graduate School revealed that job stress costs US employers more than $300 billion a year and is the fifth leading cause of death in America."[162]

Just a quarter (26%) of organisations subsidise benefits programmes for their most vulnerable populations, and only 22% offer personalised well-being programmes. Facebook's focus on ensuring that contractor wages deliver a living wage, and Amazon's efforts to raise the minimum wage for gig workers regardless of their location are examples of how companies are thinking afresh about protecting all workers' well-being.[163]

In the near future, employees will place a premium on how companies care for them. How employers respond to well-being issues like stress, burnout and uncertainty will be a hallmark of their attitude toward responsibility and sustainability. With COVID-19, employee well-being is becoming critical for organisational sustainability and employee engagement. As the definition of well-being expands, organisations now see well-being not just as an employee benefit or responsibility, but as a business performance strategy. Organisations need to recognise how fear, anxiety and fatigue can

---

161 Deloitte, 2018.
162 Mercer, 2020.
163 Mercer, 2020.

escalate when people don't feel engaged. Organisations have to include flexibility and well-being programmes as part of their long term workforce transformations.[164]

CASE STUDY: LENDLEASE

Lendlease, a multinational construction, property and infrastructure company, focuses not only on using the physical workplace to support well-being, but also on developing policies and leadership approaches that embed well-being into its culture. The company's work environment features "neighborhood" tables, working walls, focus points for activities that require concentration, and enclosed pods and breakaway areas that foster collaboration and social interaction. Lendlease's Wellness Hub, a preventative care facility that occupies two floors of its corporate headquarters, offers employees the use of dedicated rooms – the "Consultation Room", the "Contemplation Room", the "Carer's Room" and the "First Aid Room" – as well as adjoining areas, for physical activity and training. A highlight of the Wellness Hub is a six metre high breathing wall, which contains approximately 5,000 plants that accelerate the removal of air pollutants and cool the surrounding space, while also improving energy efficiency and reducing air conditioning costs. The company's leave policy includes two days during which employees can volunteer their time to a charity of personal interest. Across its international regions, Lendlease continuously rolls out well-being initiatives, including three annual well-being days and extensive health initiatives around diet and exercise that incorporate inclusive and supportive health assessment approaches.[165]

Diversity, Equity and Inclusion is becoming a key talent and cultural attractor

Recent events have propelled action from leaders on social progress. Successful organisations are powered by the diverse opinions, skill sets and life experiences of their employees. With 63% of CEOs/COOs being accountable for diversity and inclusion (D&I) metrics, D&I is one of the more

---

164 Caglar & Duarte, 2019.
165 Deloitte, 2018.

mature sustainability indices. Still, there is a need to create opportunities for women, who lag behind men in asking for promotions (60% compared to 73%) and receiving promotions and pay increases (48% compared to 62%). These disparities have a disproportionate impact on perceptions of thriving: 44% of men – but only 23% of women – who were denied a promotion reported that they are still thriving. With less than half of companies having a documented, multi-year strategy for achieving gender equality, this will be an important area for focus in 2020 and beyond.[166]

Thriving employees – defined as prospering in terms of health, wealth and career – are four times more likely to work for a company that they perceive as ensuring equity in pay/promotion decisions. Despite this, only 32% of HR leaders say that pay equity is among their top rewards priorities, although Canada (45%) and Mexico (44%) have this firmly in focus. And although 52% of companies measure pay inequity (a near fivefold increase over last year), only 12% measure how they can correct inequities moving forward. Without systemic change, truly equitable opportunities will continue to fall behind intentions. Indeed, women have unique financial challenges that are not yet being adequately addressed. If these are left unaddressed, they could have profound and disproportionate impacts on their longevity.[167]

To tap into the full potential of human diversity, organisations need to hire diverse talent and create an inclusive working culture that is underpinned by a fundamental sense of belonging, fairness and equity, enabling people to bring their "full self" to work. Recent events are a reminder of the persistent inequities that continue to pervade our societies and economies. As companies seek to take on more responsibility for addressing social justice, ensuring that diversity and equality becomes the norm in the very near future, a key pathway is to adopt an integrated approach to diversity, equity and inclusion in the workplace, and a renewed commitment to tangible change. Ensuring racial justice, gender parity, disability inclusion, LGBTQ equality and the inclusion of all forms of human diversity needs to be the "new normal" in the workplace set to emerge from the COVID-19 crisis.[168]

---

166 Mercer, 2020.
167 Mercer, 2020.
168 WEF, 2020.

WHAT COMPANIES ARE DOING TO FIGHT SYSTEMIC RACISM: PEPSICO

PepsiCo CEO: "Black Lives Matter, to our company and to me."

That's what PepsiCo CEO Ramon Laguarta wrote in his recent op-ed in *Fortune*, in which he announced a commitment of $400 million over five years to "lift up Black communities and increase Black representation at PepsiCo".

The food and beverage company's efforts will focus on three pillars: people, business and communities.

- People: PepsiCo will expand the company's Black managerial population by 30% by 2025, adding more than 250 Black associates to managerial roles. The company will also increase recruitment activities at Historically Black Colleges and Universities, establish scholarships for Black students, and mandate company-wide unconscious-bias training.

- Business: The company will double its spending with Black-owned suppliers, create more jobs for Black creators at its marketing agencies, and invest $50 million over five years to strengthen local Black-owned businesses.

- Communities: PepsiCo will invest an incremental $20 million over five years "to create opportunity and advance economic empowerment for Black Americans", including providing grants for social programmes in Black communities; providing mentorship, management training and financing for Black-owned restaurants; and supporting Black non-profit CEOs.[169]

---

169 WEF, 2020.

✍️ Checklist

1. Are you using a Talent Portfolio workforce model?

2. What do your candidates say about your recruitment and onboarding experience?

3. Have you changed your performance management and learning and development processes to fit the new world of work?

4. How are you showing you care about employee well-being and equity?

CHAPTER 6

Becoming digital- and data-driven

In this chapter, we examine how to become a digital- and data-driven HR function. There are two parts to this discussion: first, how to automate and augment critical processes so that HR can spend time on more value adding activities (Digital HR), and second, how to use data and people analytics to drive better outcomes and impact in the business.

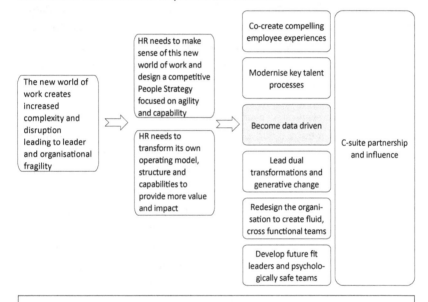

Key ideas

- Core HR processes must be automated and augmented with intelligent technology.
- HR needs to be data- and analytics-driven.

"HR professionals should become digitally and numerically literate and acquire the skills necessary to process, produce and leverage digital information. When HR professionals, as core Business Partners, are analytically and digitally more literate, they will possess skills that will put their organisation in the best possible position to deliver greater value to all stakeholders."[170]

170 Randhawa, 2020.

PART ONE: Digitalise HR

"In the HR function, we have identified more than 50% of standard HR processes that could have robotics applications."[171]

Most HR organisations spend an inordinate amount of time on manual administrative tasks. In near direct conflict with this reality is the search for ways HR can offer greater strategic contributions to their organisations. Iron Mountain has conducted a significant amount of research into how automating HR processes is a means to create the time and HR resources to move people to more strategic roles. Their results indicate that respondents from highly automated HR departments are about twice as likely to enjoy above-average productivity and considerably more likely as those from the least automated HR departments to say they enjoyed above average HR effectiveness (38% to 25%).[172]

Challenge your team to eschew paperwork and manual processes completely. This means cloud platforms, mobile apps and a social-media savviness is required from your entire team. Push them to research and find creative solutions until you have enough options to begin building your platform and connect all the dots. Don't engage with any software or systems that don't allow you to put real-time performance dashboards in place. If you're having to manually create your data analysis, that's a lot of effort being wasted on something that could or should be automated. Some of the critical technologies that HR has to get their heads around and partner with IT to deliver digital HR effectively are Robotic Process Automation (RPA) technology, Artificial Intelligence and Blockchain.

In HR, RPA technology can be used to automate activities that are rule-based, repetitive and standardised. It lends itself to where there is core data administration using an HR system, for example in payroll, on-boarding and exits. Chatbots are being used to point candidates and employees in the right direction for simple information requests such as applying for leave, i.e. they give us another tool for resolving queries alongside help-desks and HR intranets. RPA works by having a software "bot" take over high-volume, repetitive operational tasks from HR employees, often improving the accuracy and speed of data processing, such as payroll, benefits enrolment,

---

171 Deloitte, 2018.
172 French, 2019.

onboarding and compliance reporting which all require a significant amount of manual, repetitive labour. Onboarding or transferring an employee, for example, triggers multiple process steps in payroll and benefits systems that RPA bots can do, freeing up HR staff for other duties. Deloitte's 2017 Global Human Capital Trends study found that 22% of the highest-performing HR organisations are currently implementing or have implemented RPA, compared with just 6% of the lowest-performing organisations.[173] Almost half of HR global shared services executives believe RPA will deliver 10% to 20% savings to their businesses, the Deloitte survey found, with 9% expecting a savings of 40% or more.

The applications of Artificial Intelligence (AI) occur when software is using history, algorithms and data to be smarter and smarter over time. EY[174] reported that AI technologies offer significant opportunities to improve HR functions, such as self-service transactions, recruiting and talent acquisition, payroll, reporting, access policies and procedures. We are living in an era in which AI capabilities are reaching new heights and have a major impact on how we operate our businesses. Human resources executives have faith that merging AI into HR administration functions will benefit and improve the overall employee experience. This will provide more capacity, time and budget, as well as more accurate information for decisive people management.

Finding the right information, with lower costs, in less time and in a secure manner, helps to build momentum step by step, beginning with the recruitment process. From there, AI can be effectively woven into an employee's onboarding programme. New employees who may want to connect with others and get more institutional information may not know where to go. Conversational AI for the HR system will answer new employees' most pressing questions to help get them up to speed fast. For example, an AI-powered programme could provide the names, locations and contact information for people they should connect with during their first week. New employees could also be advised by AI engines to check out a new-hire web page containing useful information, including training modules and business-conduct guidelines.

In addition, conversational AI transactions can help to update personal information on behalf of the employee in a secure manner. A manager could

173 Deloitte, 2017.
174 EY, 2018.

access his or her direct report's information via a chatbot and perform HR business transactions without accessing the core HR application. Chatbots authenticate an employee and provide only authorised information for the employee to access and transact with. Conversational AI for HR transactions has a strong potential to perform certain transactions routed via an approval-chain process. For example, it can allow a manager to approve vacation requests via a chatbot, or it can provide a list of items in need of approval by the manager or HR. Managers or HR professionals would not have to access the core HR system to get KPIs and analytical data. The conversational AI solution uses a machine-learning capability – natural language processing (NLP) – to know exactly what information the employee, manager or HR professional is seeking. Note that conversational AI requires customisation; it is not easy to standardise. You can designate certain words as positive or negative, but the application works best when it can determine the correct context and the intentions of the user.[175]

Blockchain is another tool that can significantly impact the way HR is delivered. This is a distributed ledger that allows value to be exchanged securely, transparently and without risk of tampering. All parties are authorised to access the blockchain; at its root it is a trust protocol. For HR that means we can verify and assess the education, skills and performance of potential recruits, as well as support cross border payments for our global employees. Blockchain automates data-heavy processes like VAT and payroll administration, and enhances cyber security in HR. Blockchain works when processes are data-heavy and need third party verification, reducing the need for a back office as there is no need for reconciliation, receipt and other traditional components of transactions. With Blockchain processes are unified, which leads to great productivity gains. Another use of Blockchain is to keep records of employee capabilities and performance, creating a skills backpack that employees can carry with them. Which HR pain points can you address with Blockchain?[176]

If you do not have the skills in this area, it is critical that you employee data scientists and AI, robotics and automation specialists in your team, and create a strong partnership with your IT team. But it has to get done.

---

175 EY, 2018.
176 PWC, 2017.

CASE STUDY: UNILEVER

An interview with Leena Nair

David Green: When we were on stage together at CogX, I think in the UK back in June and you talked about a number of highlights a number of areas where you use technology to help improve various stages around the employee journey. So can we talk a little bit about that now, so certainly in recruitment. You've brought some technology in there. And widened the selection pool, I think.

Leena Nair: We've digitised all aspects of HR. For example, let me start with all elements of the recruitment... All elements of the employee experience every single bit.

So recruitment. Okay, we've digitised the entire recruitment process. So young graduate comes in, all he or she has to do is take a couple of seconds to put their CV from LinkedIn, play games for 24 minutes at a time of their choosing, at a place of their choosing, break it up, play a couple of games one day. No problem. Send us a selfie video for 30 minutes to 40 minutes with some standard questions. And that's it.

And then it's AI, machine learning that allows us to see who fits best at Unilever. And also then have the pool of three thousand people that we need to select the 800 graduate trainees that we have.

Now, we've two million people applying for Unilever. But now with what we're doing with digitisation we can talk to all of the two million people.

So all of the two million people get a chance to give us their CV. Play games and give us a hell of a lot of data about themselves. Interview with us. And be confident that they've had a chance to access this. In addition, every single person gets a detailed feedback about what the psychometrics were from all those steps they participated in. And that is to me the power of digital. It helps to bring scale but make it personalised. Now, you cannot worry about scale but use digitisation to break the scale up so I can provide personalisation and focus to every single person that applies for Unilever and ensure they get some feedback and ensure like they feel they had participated in the process.[177]

---

177 Green, 2020.

PART TWO: Drive impact through the use of talent and people analytics

"As the complexity of workforce challenges continues to rise, so will the demand for more quantitative approaches to address the increasingly difficult people-related questions central to organizational success. The power of workforce analytics lies in its ability to challenge conventional wisdom, influence behaviour, enable HR and business leaders to make and execute smarter workforce decisions, and ultimately, impact business outcomes. To realize value from investments in workforce analytics, organizations need to understand: the relationship between their workforce strategies and their business challenges; the approaches at their disposal; and the capabilities required to translate raw HR data into defensible action."[178]

"People analytics – defined as the use of data about human behavior, relationships and traits to make business decisions – helps to replace decision making based on anecdotal experience, hierarchy and risk avoidance with higher-quality decisions based on data analysis, prediction, and experimental research."[179]

"When the COVID-19 pandemic struck, some companies were better prepared than others to reorganize and mobilize their employees. Those organizations had effective talent analytics strategies in place."[180]

Almost two-thirds (61%) of executives say that using talent analytics to inform decision making is the number one HR trend that has delivered impact.[181] Talent and people analytics can help you change process, culture and strategy.[182] Executives argue that their companies cannot succeed without assertive, data-driven Chief Human Resources Officers (CHRO) who take a strong stance on talent issues and use research to deliver an informed point of view, according to a new report released by Visier.[183] The report surveyed 301 corporate executives at companies with revenue of $1 billion or more across America, asking their views on the changing role of

178 IBM Institute for Business Value, 2014.
179 Nielsen & McCullough, 2018.
180 Harbert, 2020.
181 Mercer, 2020.
182 Nielsen & McCullough, 2018.
183 Visier, 2020.

HR leadership. The survey found that the most sought-after CHRO is a data-driven, strategic leader who demonstrates business savvy, creativity and innovation.

Mondore et al. defined HR analytics as "demonstrating the direct impact of people data on important business outcomes".[184] In order to stay ahead of the game in people analytics, HR needs to be more 'business consultant' and less 'data analyst'. The benefits of HR departments making an investment in stronger analytics include the following:

1. They can redirect the money they spend today on the wrong employee initiatives to more beneficial employee initiatives. Specifically, those initiatives that impact critical business metrics and outcomes instead of the latest unquantified HR fads that promise to make employees happier, more engaged and satisfied.

2. The investments that they decide to make that focus on employees will result in tangible outcomes that benefit shareholders, customers and employees themselves.

3. The returns on such investments, via their impact on the top and/or bottom lines, can be quantified.

4. HR departments can be held accountable for impacting the bottom line in the same way that business or product leaders are held accountable.

5. HR executives will be included in the conversation, because they can now quantify their numerous impacts on business outcomes.

Most importantly, HR should move from opinions to actionable insights, as shown below in Figure 6.1.

---

184 Mondore et al., 2011, p. 21.

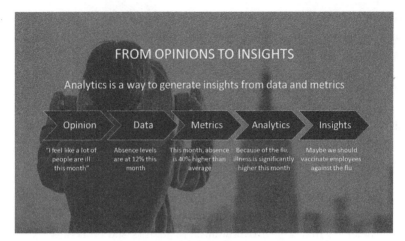

Figure 6.1: From opinions to insights[185]

HR should also deliver the analytics most requested by CEOs. Mercer[186] found that HR only delivers CEO requests between 38% and 52% of the time. Table 6.1 lists the top analytics requests from the C-suite and how well HR is responding to these requests.

Table 6.1: Top 10 analytics requests from the C-suite

	Top 10 analytics requests from the C-suite	% of HR providing today
1	Why is one team high performing and another struggling?	52%
2	What are the key drivers of engagement in our organization?	53%
3	To what extent are there pay inequities by gender and race/ethnicity?	52%
4	How do different retirement options impact older workers' bahavior?	40%
5	How are our total rewards programs being utilized by our employees?	46%
6	Who is likely to leave in the next 6-12 months?	43%
7	How can data driven insights help us understand and better manage healthcare spend globally?	41%
8	When is our critical talent likely to retire?	41%
9	Which profile of candidates tends to stay longer?	41%
10	Which populations (e.g., women, minorities) are failing to progress within the organization?	38%

185 IBM, 2014.

186 Mercer, 2020.

In order to effectively deliver analytics, Mercer[187] proposed building a cross-disciplinary team leveraging the expertise of industrial/organisational psychologists, economists, data scientists, machine learning programmers, and employee representatives. Companies like Microsoft have set up a dedicated Workplace Analytics division using people analytics in three ways: 1) in core functional or process transformation initiatives; 2) in cultural transformation initiatives; and 3) in strategic transformation.

In one example, a people analytics team at a global CPG company was enlisted to help optimise a financial process that took place monthly in every country subsidiary around the world. The diversity of local accounting rules precluded perfect standardisation, and the geographic dispersion of the teams made it hard for the transformation group to gather information the way they normally would – in conversation. So, instead of starting with discovery conversations, people analytics data was used to baseline the time spent on the process in every country, and to map the networks of the people involved. They discovered that one country was 16% percent more efficient than the average of the rest of the countries; they got the same results in 71 fewer person-hours per month and with 40 fewer people involved each month. The people analytics team was surprised – as was the finance team in that country – which had no reason to benchmark themselves against other countries and had no idea that they were such a bright spot. The transformation office approached that country's finance leaders with their findings and made them partners in a process improvement for the rest of the subsidiaries.[188]

A recent example of an organisation using people analytics to respond to COVID-19 includes a large service organisation which, pre-pandemic, had already been comprehensively collecting and coding high-quality data about the skills, capabilities, and knowledge of its employees, managers and even past applicants. When the health crisis hit, management at the firm was able to quickly identify talent and reorganise its workforce to operate successfully in a new world. If it needed more help in particular areas, it was able to hire and onboard new employees fast. It had existing technology platforms already in place that enabled it to retrain people, keep everyone connected in the age of social distancing, and give employees the right information to make fast decisions in a quickly changing environment.[189]

187 Mercer, 2020.
188 Nielsen & McCullough, 2018.
189 Harbert, 2020.

With the end-to-end digitisation of HR systems, data are pouring in from a variety of touch points, whether they are CRM systems, ATS platforms, L&D modules, or the core HRIS repository; 69% of organisations are building integrated systems to analyse worker-related data, and 17% already have real-time dashboards to crunch the avalanche of numbers in new and useful ways. But even as dashboards become a staple for any HR technology solution, a major portion of data analytics still focuses on historical records, assessments of past events, and measurement of previous performance, instead of focusing solely on the future.

Data types and sources must be evaluated for their advantages and challenges to ensure integrity and quality. Key questions to be asked include: Who entered these data, and why? How old are these data? Are there structural or technological barriers to accuracy or completeness? Could unconscious bias influence these data? How can these data be evaluated for accuracy and precision?

And what about analytics – the fine art of separating signal from noise? New analytics techniques such as network analysis, sentiment analysis, predictive analysis and artificial intelligence have the potential to add tremendous value. That being said, organisations big and small are getting 'quick wins' by simply going back to the basics. Often, simple analysis conducted thoughtfully on well-curated data sets can yield powerful results to key questions: Are people using the tools provided to them? Are people rewarded consistently and fairly? Where might employee dissatisfaction cause issues?[190]

For some, HR analytics have come down to tracking more efficiency metrics around HR activities. There is nothing wrong with measuring time-to-hire as an HR efficiency metric, but it likely does not excite your CEO – unless you have shown the direct connection between time-to-hire and the quality of people that are hired. The following leading practices should point the way for any team employing either complex or basic analytical tools:

- Invest in well-functioning systems but understand that systems are no substitute for a business-driven understanding of the situation.

- Get the right HR analytics talent in place but do not forget to utilise knowledge of the organisation to drive context.

---

190 Swift, 2018.

- Learn from data from the outside world but have a strong view on your own environment and context first.

- Benchmark but know where your organisation is unique.

- Delve into complex issues but keep outputs simple.

Emerging data sources organisations are starting to use that provide new insights into workforce issues include:

- social analytics: capturing and analysing the data generated within internal and external social platforms to better understand interactions among individuals, overall employee engagement patterns, and identify trending topics and sentiments;

- neuroscience analytics: using data collected from online cognitive tests based on neuroscience research to better understand an individual's aptitude for different types of work-related activities;

- sensor-based analytics: studying how employees move and congregate throughout the day to better understand collaboration patterns and identify sources of knowledge sharing and innovation; and

- integrated external labour market information: capturing information about local and global labour markets through mining macro-economic data, job boards, recruiting sites and other sources of public information.

CASE STUDY: MERCK

Merck believes that a leading HR function is one where analytics capability is not only for the analytics team, but the whole HR team. This does not imply that every role requires equal depth in analytics, but a new baseline of data interpretation and communication skills is critical to being effective partners to the business. To this end, they started out by democratising data within their HR community by rolling out a cloud-based workforce analytics platform. This is helping them drive greater familiarity and reliance on data among our HR users. They have also developed and deployed a capability-building programme with modules focused on metric selection, hypothesis testing, data visualisation, recommendation development, and more.

Another channel that they have been leveraging to accelerate a data driven culture in HR has been to engage members of our wider HR community as analytics "Champions". These superheroes are critical to spreading the adoption of data informed insights, since they live and breathe the daily challenges of their colleagues; and can share relatable examples with their counterparts on how data can unlock value.

Merck's formal workforce analytics team (WFA) has 15 members who support 69,000 employees in over 80 markets worldwide through a rich portfolio of people analytics products.

The team consists of three primary pillars: Consulting, Advanced Analytics, and Reporting & Data Visualisation (see Figure 6.2 below).

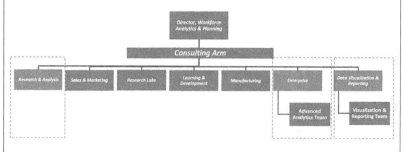

Figure 6.2: The Merck Workforce and Analytics Team structure[191]

CASE STUDY: NAB

NAB is a financial services organisation established 160 years ago in Australia. They have more than 30,000 people serving 9,000,000 customers at more than 900 locations in Australia, New Zealand and around the world.

NAB is applying analytics to benefit its 40,000-strong workforce, using data and insights to identify high-performing individuals, teams and branches, and find ways to replicate that success at scale. The bank has embraced 'people analytics', a discipline that combines "analytics, employee experience and HR technology," says people analytics general manager Thomas Hedegaard Rasmussen.

191 Green & Gamel, 2018.

People analytics has risen to prominence as large organisations try to work out how to make customers happier and grow shareholder value. "We have an abundance of research showing that if you treat your employees well, they will take care of your customers and that will take care of your shareholders," Rasmussen said.

Rasmussen said it took a year of internal lobbying for NAB to properly embrace people analytics. He said technology was important to running people analytics at scale, enabling the bank to move from initiatives impacting "a few hundred people at a time" to work that impacted the bank's entire 40,000-strong workforce.

"That's what I think is truly exciting about technology," he said. "And that [scale] actually also then gives us data that we can feed back into the process. "In one project, the bank sought to identify which of its "roughly 1000 branches spread across Australia" had the highest customer satisfaction, and why this was the case.

"We have more than 10 years of really good data – at a branch level, individual level, customer satisfaction scores, sales results, repeat revenue, income etc., and we [also] had all of this HR data," Rasmussen said. By combining and analysing the data, Rasmussen said, "a clear picture emerges". "In branches where we have the highest employee engagement, the customer satisfaction is twice as high," he said. "So if our people get the feeling that we don't care about them, they are not going to care about our customers. That's essentially what we're finding.

"We also looked at what that means in terms of NAB's money. So in an average year, NAB gets a profit of around $5-6 billion – depending on multiple things, of course, but that's what it's been like historically – and we can see that employee motivation accounts for around a billion [of that]. So that's the monetary value of it." Rasmussen said the data had helped neutralise "chicken and egg conversations" internally at the executive level on how to grow customer engagement and shareholder value.[192]

192 Crozier, 2020.

CASE STUDY: CREDIT SUISSE

On March 13 2015, the *Wall Street Journal* published an article titled: "The Algorithm That Tells the Boss Who Might Quit". The article explored how Credit Suisse was able to predict who might quit the company. It was one of the first examples of the now very popular employee churn analytics.

Not only were the analysts at Credit Suisse able to predict who might quit, but they also could identify why these people might quit. This information was provided anonymously to managers so they could reduce turnover risk factors and retain their people better.

In addition, special managers were trained to retain the high performing employees who had a high flight risk. In total, this programme saved Credit Suisse approximately $70,000,000 a year.[193]

☑ Checklist

1. How effectively are you using RPA, AI and blockchain to digitise your HR processes?

2. What are the key activities within this role that could be automated to provide greater efficiency and effectiveness to accomplish routine tasks?

3. What are the business processes that are painful and involve a lot of people, shared data, time and risk?

4. How could more value be created by applying people analytics to identify new business insights for better strategic planning and actions?

5. Have you got the right capabilities to deliver digital- and data-driven HR?

---

193 van Vulpen, 2019.

CHAPTER 7

Leading dual transformations and generative change

Human Resources and Organisation Development have a key role to play in leading and partnering with the Board and C-suite in organisational transformations and generative change to renew cultures and move the organisation and employees from fragile to agile (and even anti-fragile). This chapter will examine the methods needed to deliver these types of change and transformation initiatives effectively.

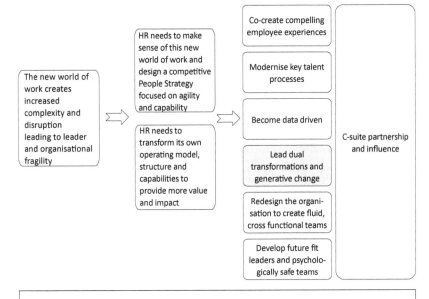

Key ideas

- Organisation transformation and resilience is a partnership between OD, HR and the C-suite.
- Dual and always on transformation is the way to go.
- Organisation Development (OD) needs to use dialogic and generative methods.

Organisation transformation and resilience is a partnership between OD, HR and the C-suite

"Organizational resilience starts at the top. If disaster and recovery have been left to Human Resources, the COVID-19 experience should make you revisit that strategy."[194]

"Well-led businesses survive. Indeed, they strengthen their recovery because their resilience has legs. Resilient organizations are fluid and flexible. They are people and purpose-driven and ready to adapt to change before procedures are taxed."[195]

"As the world becomes increasingly complex we need leaders that are increasingly complex. That's one of the reasons OD is re-emerging and gaining more profile. It's this recognition of the need for human development past the stage that was effective for bureaucratic organising, to ones that are networked and more organically run".[196]

"If you don't transform... if you don't reinvent yourself, change your organisation structure; if you don't talk about speed of innovation – you're going to get disrupted. And it'll be a brutal disruption, where the majority of companies will not exist in a meaningful way 10 to 15 years from now."[197]

Research shows that corporate lifespans are shrinking, and that half of today's S&P 500 companies will be replaced over the next 10 years. COVID-19 has exposed even more fragilities in organisations. What is the role of OD and HR in all of this? The job of OD practitioners is to build adaptive and anti-fragile organisations in partnership with the C-suite; systems needs a certain amount of stress and disorder in order to grow.[198]

Is your organisation fragile or anti-fragile? Fragile organisations have these characteristics:

---

194 Carter, 2020.
195 Carter, 2020.
196 Bushe, 2018 (in Roper)
197 John Chambers, 2018 (in Plexus Institute).
198 Taleb, 2014.

1. They do not know they are fragile: there is an overall low level of awareness in the organisation. Anti-fragile organisations know their own potential fragility.

2. Not being joined up: they are disjointed between vision, leadership, communication, strategy and objectives, and struggle to respond to stresses as a result.

3. Knowing, not doing: they know they are fragile, but do nothing about it.

4. They do risk management incorrectly: risk is only about compliance.

5. Too much emphasis on money and short termism: a sole focus on money distorts their decision making.

6. Bureaucracy and emphasis on control: people are disempowered and following rules and procedures. There is low flexibility and agility.

7. Badly managed change: leading ongoing change is key to anti-fragility, so the absence or poor management of it indicates fragility.

8. Weak processes or emphasis on initiatives: complacency and hard-wired processes create fragility.

9. Non-transparent decision making: unclear decision making can increase inaction.

10. Naïve offshoring and ignoring customers: offshoring without safeguards for quality issues and disruptions, as well as paying insufficient attention to the customer, creates fragility.

Anti-fragile organisations have the following characteristics:

- Ability to learn fast in an emergency, contain it and apply their learning.
- Preoccupation with failure.
- Reluctance to simplify interpretations.
- Sensitivity to operations.
- Commitment to resilience.
- Deference to expertise.[199]

---

199 Bendell, 2014.

Transforming and building anti-fragile organisations starts with the commitment of the CEO as the Chief Change Agent. Berardino et al.[200] wrote that, "The entire organization, whether it's 5,000, 50,000 or 500,000 associates, is looking at the CEO to determine if they are fully committed to the change required to transform the enterprise. Whether they want to assume the role or not, they are seen as leader of the change". To carry out a long term, sustainable transformation, CEOs must make clear that the transformation is essential to the enterprise's success, signal that the change required is non-negotiable, and they must stay the course through the toughest times. Once a transformation plan has been developed, a coinciding change management plan must be established by the chief human resources officer (CHRO) and his or her OD/Change team. When a CEO takes on the role of leading change, it does not undermine the critical role of the CHRO or Change Management team – rather, these expert resources should shape plans that position the CEO as a highly visible leader of the change.

CEOs must also hold their senior leadership team equally accountable for managing and leading change. The CEO must have the courage to identify and tackle head-on barriers to change that could undermine or derail the transformation. The CHRO has a crucial role to play in supporting the CEO in carrying out all of these actions. They need to actively coach the CEO on how to lead change, providing continuous guidance and feedback in one-on-one sessions. More importantly, the CEO must be willing to embrace the coaching; s/he cannot play the change agent role effectively without leveraging their CHRO as a trust-based advisor.

CASE STUDY: MICROSOFT

CPO Kathleen Hogan talks to Ron Carucci

Microsoft spent nine months in deep, engaged listening across the organization. Says Hogan, "We spoke with experts, senior leaders and VPs, and numerous focus groups with a wide variety of diverse employee groups to learn about their experience, the culture they desired, what we were passionate about preserving from our history, and what we needed to leave behind."

---

200 Berardino et al., 2019.

When they were done, they had more than 50 different ways to describe their aspirations. They assembled a "culture cabinet" to boil it down to simple statements and act as evangelists to roll it out. These statements embodied the Growth Mindset they wanted to embed – being customer obsessed, diverse and inclusive, and to accrue up to one Microsoft. Hogan says, "Together, these would allow us to make the difference we wanted to make in the world." Microsoft's history of taking on bold technological challenges with real impact, and giving back to the world, were examples of cultural attributes they desired to retain. But a highly individualistic and internally competitive culture that feared failure, struggled to collaborate, and as Nadella called it, a culture of "know it all's," were attributes it was time to shed. Says Hogan, "We knew we couldn't just put out dogma or platitudes. It takes time to tap into something people really care about and want to achieve. That power has real teeth. If people recognize your final destination as someplace they want to go, they will help you get there."

Says Hogan, "We leveraged our technological DNA. We collect daily pulse data from employees to gain real-time insights about their experience and where we are falling short. We also use data to help disconfirm unfolding misperceptions." Beyond tracking progress, the use of honest data has a secondary benefit. Acknowledging shortfalls about culture efforts further enables change. In a culture where people struggle to admit they don't know something, calculating risk can be tricky. Hogan says, "Being open about failure helps us balance a growth mindset with accountability. We are learning to not just reward success, but also reward people who fell short while getting us closer. We don't need people to show up in meetings having memorized pages of information to look smart. We want it to be perfectly acceptable to say, 'I don't have that information, but I can get it.' Learning from our mistakes gets us closer to our desired results –that's a new form of accountability for us. That's the journey."

Hogan shared her personal experience of this. She and her HR team mis-stepped on the rollout of an HR programme. She anxiously approached her boss, Nadella, about how to handle it. She'd drafted an email apologising to employees with a plan for how she and her team would rectify the problem. She reflected, "I'm not in the habit of having my boss proofread my emails, and I was uneasy about how he might respond to the mistake we'd made. My team was down the hall equally anxious about what I would hear. But Satya just said, 'You're overly apologetic. You've acknowledged the mistake, stated what you've learned and how you intend to fix it. Now move on.' I felt like a huge weight was lifted." How leaders act in tough moments when someone skins their knees shapes how a culture treats failure and learning.

Ground culture change in purpose. It's not news that employees today want to know their contributions are making a difference. Nadella has stated that he wants every Microsoft employee to discover a deep sense of purpose in their work. Many well-intentioned culture change efforts set out to reach and inspire all employees. But "reaching" and "inspiring" can translate to mere momentary interactions lacking sustainable engagement. Says Hogan, "We are trying to enlist every one of our 140,000 employees in this effort. We need them. We've activated our 18,000 managers with tools and approaches to help them engage their teams. In hindsight, I wish we'd done even more to engage managers – the role of leaders can't be overstated. They have to embody the culture. Having Satya as an amazing role model has made a huge difference."

Hogan described a leadership offsite where Nadella's team sat casually on couches (vs. a conference table) talking about their own sense of purpose in the world, and how they hoped the Microsoft platform would enable them to realize it. Hogan says, "That ability to connect our own purpose to the mission sustains us. When you can zoom out and see how we are making a difference, that's energizing in the face of the day to day challenges. We're feeling like a united team more than ever. While strategy will evolve, your culture and sense of purpose should be long-lasting. Culture paired with a purpose-driven mission allows your employees to use your company platform to realize their own aspirations and passions." And they've cascaded that down through the organization. The Microsoft annual meeting used to be a global, five-day barrage of presentations "talking at" people, but has been repurposed to include a "hackathon," with highly interactive product expos and learning sessions. The more engaged in change people are, the more they believe their contributions matter, resulting in a genuine sense of purpose.

Integrate multiple levers. The most successful culture change efforts choreograph a set of integrated activities around the levers that shape people's behaviour. Communication practices, strategy and resource allocation processes, and the full gamut of HR activities from hiring to rewards and promotion, all play vital roles in changing behaviour. But too many culture change efforts fail to pull these levers in a holistic fashion, strafing the organisation with random, disconnected efforts that work at cross-purposes and confuse employees. Hogan says, "You have to embed culture change into who you are. We've shifted our performance review emphasis on individual contribution to a more balanced focus that adds contribution to others (collaborating and helping) and leveraging others (asking for help and building on other's ideas). By evaluating and rewarding a more cohesive set of behaviours, people are learning to work more collaboratively." Microsoft has also built a new leadership platform focused on developing leaders who "model, coach and care." Together, these shifts in performance focus are helping leaders and employees change how they contribute. Hogan has also overhauled hiring practices from "screening out to screening in," creating a more inclusive and diverse workforce. They used to hire from only a few top universities, but now recruit top talent from more than 500 universities.

Consistent and constant communication has also been critical. While many organizations ratchet up "information disbursement" during culture change that do little more than clog inboxes, Microsoft figured out that people feel communicated to when they are talking. For example, employees are able to join (in person or virtually) Nadella's monthly Q&A to hear from him as well as ask direct questions. Through Yammer and Skype, they give real-time feedback, which helps leaders understand what resonates and what doesn't. Says Hogan, "There are no silver bullets. You can't have a 'favourite' culture lever, or over index on any one tactic. Culture change is a complex set of levers that you have to pull in concert. Be prepared for three steps forward, two steps back. It's a learning journey."

Shape the narrative. Successful culture change is an epic story within the larger context of the organization's past and future chapters. The stories you do, and don't tell create the folklore and legend that transmit through the organization. Soon into his time as CEO, Nadella instituted a practice on his team called "research of the amazing." At each Friday's leadership meeting, one member of the team is responsible for researching a story from somewhere in the Microsoft ecosystem of employees doing amazing things and embodying the aspired culture. They discovered stories like an innovation director at Microsoft's Cambridge R&D lab whose compassion led to developing a hand-stabilizing watch for a women suffering with Parkinson's disease. They've heard stories of employees helping customers transform business models, enabling more efficient cancer research and helping teachers be more effective in their classrooms.

Says Hogan, "We now have almost five years of weekly stories about living our purpose to make a difference while embodying our culture. Can you imagine how that many stories have shaped the narrative of our culture?" Of course, this doesn't mean ignoring stories of cultural failure. But in the face of difficult challenges and cultural setbacks, having a bounty of representative stories helps fuel leaders with needed energy during protracted seasons of change. Importantly, the narrative around you has to reconcile with the narrative within you. Says Hogan, "One of the hardest parts of the journey is hearing stories where we've failed to live up to our aspired culture – where an employee's experience didn't match what we've promised. We all want Microsoft to be an exceptional place to work, and when we fail, it's painful. I also know that with 140,000 employees, no matter what decision I make, I'm going to disappoint someone. That's the reality of leadership. I have to stay centered on what we're trying to accomplish, remain grateful and grounded in my own purpose, and on days we fall short, let my inner yardstick be the narrative that helps me see the forest for the trees." No change effort goes unopposed. There will always be critics on the sidelines jeering about how your change isn't working. Prevent those voices from hijacking the story of your culture journey by proactively narrating the entire story for the organization.

> Stay humble. No leader embarks on cultural transformation prepared for its gruelling requirements. Many cover up feelings of fear and inadequacy with contrived confidence, or prematurely declare victory at the smallest sign of change. Humility is a powerful antidote to these traps. Says Hogan, "You're never done. Culture is something you have to earn every day and you're only as good as your last day. But the greatest joy I have is seeing people being their authentic self, bringing their A game, and being their best self. That's the privilege of this role." But Hogan reflects that it didn't start that way. As a seasoned executive leading Microsoft's services business, she didn't grow up in HR. She says, "The steep learning curve kept me humble. I had to surround myself with technical experts in HR who complimented what I didn't bring to the table. I spent time with my industry CHRO peers learning how they onboarded into their roles. I had a lot to learn, and there's lots more to learn."[201]

Dual and "always on" transformation is the way to go

"Unprecedented disruption and market turbulence, coupled with the aspirations of leaders to reach higher, require organizations to launch more-frequent transformations, often of different types, with several underway at any given time. We are in an era of 'always on' transformation."[202]

"In order to survive in the increasingly frenetic, rapidly evolving world of business, organizations must disrupt or be disrupted — even when that means disrupting your own business."[203]

We are in a new era of "always on" transformation (see Figure 7.1), in which companies no longer launch individual transformations but are, in effect, always transforming. In practice, this means that a company will have several transformations of various types underway, at various stages, each building upon – and often interconnected with – the others. Executed well, these will combine to take the company to successively higher levels of performance.

---

201 Carrucci, 2014.
202 BCG, 2016.
203 Innov8rs, 2018.

The right response to disruptive threats is a two-track process to make today's business more resilient while creating tomorrow's new growth business.[204, 205]

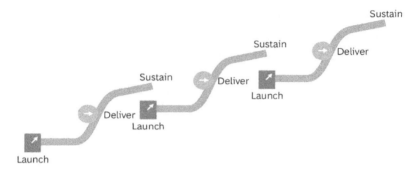

Figure 7.1: "Always on" transformation[206]

Many firms that have tried to transform have failed. A common reason for this is that leaders approach the change as one monolithic process, during which the old company becomes a new one. In this "always on" transformation, the organisation is running at two speeds at the same time and using emergence as a principle. Success requires repositioning the core business while actively investing in the new growth business using adaptive space.[207]

For organisations to be agile, they need to openly scan across and beyond themselves for the next big thing, then they need to think about how to bring an idea into the world in a more tangible manner. Finally, they need to scale these concepts throughout their organisations to enable a new normal by positively disrupting themselves. Adaptive space can be thought of as the relational and emotional freedom for people to freely explore, exchange and debate ideas. It operates as a sort of free-trade zone for ideas; by tapping into the power of network dynamics, adaptive space creates connections that serve to discover, develop and diffuse new ideas into and across an organisation.[208] This is shown in Figure 7.2.

---

204 BCG, 2016.

205 Anthony et al., 2017.

206 BCG, 2016.

207 Uhl-Bien & Arena, 2016.

208 Plexus Institute, 2018.

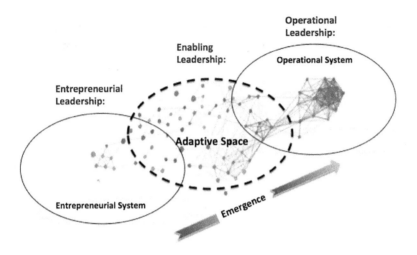

Figure 7.2: Adaptive space bridging the two systems[209]

CASE STUDY: GENERAL MOTORS

After more than 100 years as a traditional automotive manufacturer, General Motors began to realize that it needed to make changes to remain a competitive force in the industry. Once the largest automotive manufacturer in the world, it was no longer making a profit as of 2005.

The 2008 global financial crisis – when car sales plunged – only increased its losses. With liabilities twice its assets in 2009, GM engaged in an ongoing process of improving the operating cost of its core business by reducing the number of employees, closing factories, and shedding dealers.

It likewise began to reinvent itself as a completely different kind of company – one that could create its future and adapt quickly to change. The transportation industry was beginning to rapidly evolve, and this meant GM would need talents and skill sets that were uncommon for traditional automotive employees. Central to its reinvention efforts, the auto manufacturer wanted to create a new corporate culture that would foster positive disruption from within and redefine the future of mobility.

---

209 Arena & Uhl-Bien, 2016.

So in 2012, GM brought on Michael Arena as its chief talent officer to support the company's new direction. Arena's group launched GM 2020, built on principles of adaptive space and network theory. Its purpose was to energize employees to reinvent the company culture from within.

"I was brought on at GM to work on things such as engagement and refreshing the talent pool. Culture was certainly in my purview, but I wasn't asked to reinvent it. GM 2020 was more of an organic movement that emerged from within with only a little nudge from me. I sponsored it, but I didn't lead it."

Arena adds, "Instead of architecting or designing the future ourselves, we decided to invite a few people in the organisation to help us. We picked 30 young folks who had joined the company within the previous six months and asked if they would co-create the future with us."

The young employees decided that middle managers needed to be part of the co-creation, so they picked 30 middle managers and invited them into the group. Arena's team organized a design thinking boot camp to help them look at the challenge of positive disruption.

The group of 60 people chose to continue their learning by visiting environments in Detroit, Michigan, that they thought were already progressive. That spurred discussions about what paradigms at GM needed to be shed to move forward.

Arena's group also commissioned a study by futurists deep within GM. They identified four factors that would need to be true of GM's culture in the future if it were going to succeed:

- Purpose. People want to be part of something related to a purpose. They want to work where there is an innovation imperative to which they feel they are contributing.

- Growth. They want to feel they are part of something they are helping to grow and that helps them grow as a result.

- Connectivity. They want to be part of something that's extensively connected but not complex.

- People development. There would need to be activity and investment around people development, because the new culture would reveal a shortage of skill sets needed for future success.

"These characteristics are commonplace today, but they weren't in 2013," says Arena. The grassroots movement of GM 2020 grew organically, eventually attracting almost 5,000 employees to the task of disrupting and reinventing GM's culture. Participation is voluntary, and the group is self-organizing.

"These people have become a tremendous catalyst for change across the company," Arena explains. "They're challenging us to think about the future of work and what it means to be innovative and agile. They look at everything from space configuration to where we should invest resources to what type of culture we want."

Arena describes GM Chairman and CEO Mary Barra as "the chief energizing ion who fires people up about a future that's different. In October 2017, she announced our vision of a future with zero crashes, zero emissions, and zero congestion. Barra's leadership is drawing together like-minded people to take on these really big challenges."[210]

Anthony et al.[211] developed a dual transformation formula for organisations to use to simultaneously lower costs in the core and reposition the core business, whilst creating a future disruptive business and using core strengths and capabilities to link the two. This helps the organisation to be both reliable and agile, and bring the two-speed process to life. This approach is set out in Figure 7.3.

---

210 Gallaghan, 2018.
211 Anthony et al., 2017.

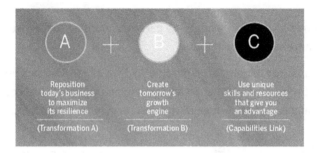

Figure 7.3: Dual transformation

Examples of Transformation A are Adobe moving from packaged software to a subscription model, and Netflix moving from rentals to subscriptions and from DVDs to streaming. The essence is changing the HOW. Find more effective ways to address customer needs to maximise the resilience and relevance of your core business.

Examples of Transformation B are Alphabet moving from being a search engine to advertising, SingPost moving from mail delivery to logistics services, and Amazon moving from retailer to cloud computing leader. Here you change WHAT you do and find new ways to solve a different problem. Use partnerships, acquisitions and external hires to accelerate the capabilities needed and iteratively develop the business model.

The most difficult part of a dual transformation is the wise use of the company's skills and resources: leveraging valuable assets like brand, distribution and accumulated know-how to build the new growth engine the company needs. This "capabilities link" is a bridge from the company of today to the growth leader of tomorrow.

Yet ultimately, dual transformation is about a change in mindsets and behaviours. When making large-scale organisational changes, the design of a transformation's initiatives is not a matter of guesswork. Rather, the results from a new McKinsey Global Survey on the topic suggest that companies that design their initiatives to support desired shifts in mind-sets and behaviours see the most successful transformations.[212]

---

212 McKinsey, 2015.

CASE STUDY: JOHNSON & JOHNSON

Johnson & Johnson (J&J) is a global health company with 120,000 employees in 57 countries. They use dual transformation when transforming and growing the organisation. Below is one such example:[213]

TRANSFORMATION A:
- J&J centralized pharma operations under Janssen.
- Narrowed the R&D portfolio from 33 disease areas to 13.
- Dispensed with the "not invented here" bias; partnered with outside institutions.
- Developed "disease strongholds" and amassed industry-leading expertise.

TRANSFORMATION B:
- Adopted a new focus: stopping the causes of disease (i.e., "disease interception").
- A new "accelerator" unit developed treatments to stop disease-causing processes (e.g., juvenile diabetes).
- New disease intervention models will require substantial business model innovation: e.g., different diagnostic, consumer products and other interventions that are very different from the traditional drug model.

CAPABILITIES LINK:
- Janssen's scientific expertise, the access of its sales force, the door-opening power of its global brand, and its purpose and mission.

OD – you need to use dialogic and generative methods

"A lot of people think they're doing OD but they're doing it without the 'O'. They have elements of OD and even embrace OD values... but there's no strategic content. So you've really engaged people with the change, but you haven't investigated what needs to change from the customer's point of view, you haven't benchmarked the competitive position of the organisation..."[214]

---

213 Anthony et al., 2017.
214 Cheung-Judge, 2018 (in Roper).

"Our definition of OD at the NHS is we're about enabling people to transform systems."[215]

"The dominant diagnostic mindset views organizations as systems and processes that can be woven into a structure suited to a particular environment. Dialogic mindset sees organizations as ongoing conversations in which the organisation is constantly influenced by who talks to whom about what. Organizations are stories. When you change the story, you change the world."[216]

"Diagnosis at best can only capture a moment in time and in today's world of rapid and constant change it inherently provides an out of date picture for the client system to work with. By the time contracting is completed, a diagnostic process initiated, data collected, responses prepared for presentation, and a feedback session conducted conditions could have shifted in important ways. This has always been a limitation of the data-feedback model, but it has become an increasing concern with the shift to today's world of hyper- active systems and continuous change."[217]

"Patterns and stories may continue in a self-perpetuating cycle until a conscious choice is made to examine the links and choose to think or act differently. In this sense, once cyclical stories and patterns become embedded, they are self- sustaining and can result in thoughts and feelings of being stuck, whereas consciously engaging in mutual dialogue regarding the links and opportunities to think or act differently holds generative potential for whole system transformation."[218]

For OD to remain relevant and impactful in a world of "always on", dual transformation and adaptive spaces, practitioners need to evolve their methods and capabilities. Planned and diagnostic methods no longer work in increasingly complex and fast changing environments. What is needed are dialogic and generative approaches that are co-created with stakeholders and that evolve over time.

---

215 Taylor-Pitt, 2018 (in Roper).
216 CHO Group, 2015.
217 Bushe & Marshak, 2013.
218 Bushe & Marshak, 2013.

The roots of planned change in OD were planted early and run deep. Kurt Lewin considered his seminal approach to social change to be a form of planned change or social engineering. For Lewin and his followers, identifying what conditions needed to be changed, and the means to change them to bring about a given result, involved conceptualising behaviour as a function of a field of forces that could be diagnosed and acted upon with targeted interventions to create movement towards a desired change goal. Change management models are evolving fast from planned change to generative change based on emergence and narratives. Generative change theory is based on different premises from those in planned change theory.

These premises are described below:

- An organisational dilemma, disruption or compelling desire triggers a search for new "adaptive moves" that are different from current ways of thinking.

- Leadership recognises the systemic context of the situation, is future focused, and is open to possibility-centric framings of the issue.

- Leadership is willing to enlist and engage a range of stakeholders in interactions and inquiry, with a purpose but not a goal or specific outcome in mind.

- The current state is presumed to be fluid with the prevailing narrative(s) that guides thought, and action being continuously socially constructed through ongoing conversations and social interactions.

- A diversity of perspectives and narratives are enlisted and encouraged within safe containers to help challenge prevailing narratives and provide new insights, awareness and possibilities.

- New ideas, creative possibilities, generative images and new shared narrative(s) emerge from those interactions, stimulated, framed and guided by generative leadership.

- Change occurs through experimentation and iterative moves as emergent strategies, probes, and new adaptive ways of thinking and acting are carried out by participants throughout the system.

Because dialogic practices support the people who make up a system to interact creatively around complex, important issues, they generate new ideas and connections, and inspire agreements to act around emerging shared aspirations. A common result of continued use is a shift in the cultural narrative that shapes the way people see their personal and collective identities. This basic approach to generative change in OD utilises a variety of methods for creating containers where new kinds of conversations can take place, but generally has the following steps: entry and contracting; identification of a purpose that is future focused and possibility-centric; the engagement of diverse stakeholders in ways that generate new conversations; the stimulation of self-organised innovations amongst those stakeholders; leadership actions that monitor, scale up and embed promising innovations; and learnings from success and failures lead to new adaptive moves.

Diagnostic OD positions diagnosis, an outcome of data gathering, as an essential stage in the consultancy process, occurring in time prior to intervention. Dialogic OD, on the other hand, treats meaning making as an ongoing and integrated dimension of the interactive process. Organisations are meaning-making systems; it is all about human processes and systems views. The key outcome of successful OD interventions should be increased organisational agility and resilience, and it is moving increasingly from diagnostic to dialogic approaches as complexity requires more dialogue.[219]

Organisational actors partially create their reality through the retrospective stories they tell about their experience and the future-oriented stories they create as a pathway to action. Convergence of narratives by organisation members drive collective sense making. Broadly speaking, diagnostic OD emerged to improve the functioning of overly bounded, hierarchical organisations by thinking of them as living, open systems. Starting in the 1980s and accelerating into the present, OD has been influenced by developments in the social, biological and physical sciences, as well as newer interventions and approaches to change created by innovative practitioners. These include social construction, the complexity sciences, the linguistic turn in the social sciences, appreciative inquiry, and large group methods. A basic assumption of dialogic OD practices is that change occurs through changing the conversations in a system.

Dialogic OD can utilise any number of techniques during events that engage as many members of the community as possible, rapidly, in one or more new conversations. A common image used to describe dialogic OD events is the

219 Bushe & Marshak, 2018.

creation of a container: a time and space where normal, business-as-usual ways of interacting are suspended so that different, generative conversations can take place. At some point the dialogic OD process shifts from stimulating ideas through generative images to launching action (probes). After the events, change is facilitated by people in the community tracking the actual changes taking place and supporting sponsors in recognising and amplifying desired changes (sensing and responding to successful probes).

A POWERFUL DIALOGICAL OD TOOL: ADAPTIVE ACTION

Adaptive Action is an elegant and powerful method for engaging with dynamic change in an ever-emerging, always self-organising world. Adaptive Action is a cycle; an adaptive actor always stands in inquiry, and every ending action makes the next beginning question necessary. The Adaptive Action model consists of three questions:

- What? What do you see? What changes have occurred? What is the same as before? What is different? What containers are most relevant? What differences are emerging or disappearing? What are the current exchanges and how strong are they? What is the pattern of the past? What desires are there for patterns in the future?

- So what? So what surprises you? So what do your observations mean to you? So what do they mean to others? So what might you expect in future? So what assumptions or expectations were confirmed or denied? So what containers are open to change, and what might those changes mean? So what differences are open to change, and how might new or more effective differences be infused into the system? So what options are there for building new exchanges, changing existing ones, or breaking ones that are not helpful?

- Now what? Now what will I do? Now what will you do? Now what will we do together? Now what messages should we send to others? Now what outcomes might we expect? Now what will we do to collect data for our next and emerging cycle?[220]

---

220 Eoyang & Holladay, 2013.

Other dialogic methods are seen in Table 7.1 below.

1. Art of Convening (Neal & Neal)
2. Art of Hosting (artofhosting.org)
3. Appreciative Inquiry (Cooperrider)
4. Complex Responsive Processes (Stacey, Shaw)
5. Conference Model (Axelrod)
6. Coordinated Management of Meaning (Pearce & Cronen)
7. Cycle of Resolution (Levine)
8. Dynamic Facilitation (Rough)
9. Engaging Emergence (Holman)
10. Future Search (Weisbord)
11. Narrative Mediation (Winslade & Monk)
12. Open Space Technology (Owen)
13. Organizational Learning Conversations (Bushe)
14. Reflexive Inquiry (Oliver)
15. Real Time Strategic Change (Jacobs)
16. Re-description (Storch)
17. Search Conference (Emery)
18. Solution Focused Dialogue (Jackson & McKergow)
19. Structure of Belonging (Block)
20. Syntegration (Beer)
21. Systemic Sustainability (Amadeo & Cox)
22. Talking Stick (pre-industrial)
23. Technology of Participation (Spencer)
24. The Circle Way (Baldwin)
25. Visual Explorer (Palus & Horth)
26. Work Out (Ashkenas)
27. World Café (Brown & Isaacs)

Table 7.1: Dialogic OD methods[221]

---

221 Bushe & Marshak, 2013.

CASE STUDY: BIOTECH FIRM

A biotech company was building a new facility. The regional director saw an opportunity to find synergies across departmental divides in anticipation of moving from separate buildings into a shared space.

As part of the process, they convened an Open Space Technology meeting, bringing together about 100 people from all parts of the region. Open Space Technology invites people to self-organise around what they love in order to address complex, important issues (Holman, 2010). At the close of the first day of the gathering, one participant characterised the experience by saying that she had worked for the company for years and finally left out of frustration. She returned a few months ago after five years away to find that not one of the issues that had frustrated her had changed. She declared that by the time this unprecedented meeting ended, those issues would be addressed. That declaration became a rallying cry, as others echoed both her frustration and their determination to break ingrained, unproductive habits. By the end of the event, not only had people handled long-standing issues, they developed a deeper understanding of how interconnected they were that would serve them in moving forward.

By using a dialogic practice, this company broke through ingrained habit to begin developing new relationships for shared purposes. Now imagine if more of our work left more capable, engaged systems in their wake.[222]

When we use dialogic practices to engage the people of a system in conversations that address their own issues, we not only solve the immediate problem, but we leave behind a more evolved system, with a greater sense of direction and hope of personal connection, and the energy and will to work across previously unbridgeable boundaries.

Bushe and Marshak[223] wrote that Organisational Development (OD) has long been associated, if not synonymous, with planned change. Generative change works with dialogic processes when there is a lot of complexity to

---

222 Bushe & Marshak, 2013.
223 Bushe & Marshak, 2018.

be dealt with, and requires identifying the issue or problem that needs to be addressed and framing it in a way that will motivate the variety of stakeholders who are "part of the problem" to engage in coming up with new ideas. They are invited into conversations intended to stimulate many self-initiated, fail-safe innovations and see what works. Those innovations that do work are then nurtured and scaled up. Rather than saying, "I know the answer, follow me", generative leaders say, "I know the challenge, and I invite you to decide what you will do about it".

Organisations are conceived to be complex, responsive, meaning-making systems, wherein narratives, stories, metaphors and conversations continuously construct social reality through the day-to-day interactions of organisational members. Diagnosis of problems is eschewed in favour of inquiry and generative processes that help stimulate the emergence of new and potentially transformational insights and possibilities that are especially needed when facing highly complex, novel organisational challenges. Leaders and consultants can help foster, support and/or accelerate the emergence of transformational possibilities by encouraging disruptions to taken-for-granted ways of thinking and acting and the use of generative images to stimulate new conversations and narratives. Because social reality continuously emerges through any and all interactions, the consultant is always part of the unfolding processes of stability and change rather than a neutral facilitator who stands apart from the system.

Generative change theory is based on different premises from those in planned change theory. These premises include the below:

- An organisational dilemma, disruption or compelling desire triggers a search for new "adaptive moves" that are different from current ways of thinking.

- Leadership recognises the systemic context of the situation, is future focused, and is open to possibility-centric framings of the issue.

- Leadership is willing to enlist and engage a range of stakeholders in interactions and inquiry, with a purpose but not a goal or specific outcome in mind.

- The current state is presumed to be fluid with the prevailing narrative(s) that guides thought, and action being continuously socially constructed through ongoing conversations and social interactions.

- A diversity of perspectives and narratives are enlisted and encouraged within safe containers to help challenge prevailing narratives and provide new insights, awareness and possibilities.

- New ideas, creative possibilities, generative images and new shared narrative(s) emerge from those interactions stimulated, framed and guided by generative leadership.

- Change occurs through experimentation and iterative moves as emergent strategies, probes, and new adaptive ways of thinking and acting are carried out by participants throughout the system.

- Leadership assesses the systemic factors and forces impacting the situation and focuses not on identifying and directing the change, but on leading the processes of emergent change with special attention given to modelling, nurturing, and embedding changes that prove successful in a learn as you go approach.

- The change agent partners with the system providing collaborative consultation but not expert solutions. Furthermore, the change agent is considered to be part of the ongoing social construction of reality and not able to stand apart from it as a neutral, objective actor.

The generative change process is shown below in Figure 7.4.

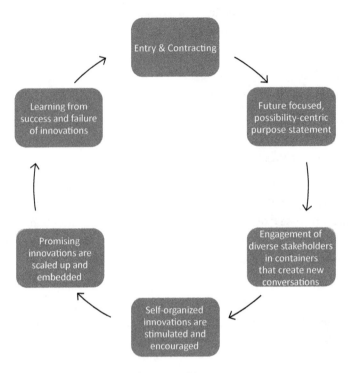

Figure 7.4: OD generative change in practice[224]

Narratives are sources of stability and change in organisations. We need to understand current dominant and emerging narratives, and develop useful and realistic narratives that support change. A single narrative rarely captures the change. Given the ambiguity during change, narratives can label organisational events in important ways. Different narratives, advanced by varying constituents with their own interests, can portray and shape others' interpretations of the events unfolding around them. In other words, narratives have tremendous power as an organisational scorekeeper; they socially construct success and failures of change initiatives.[225] Generative images are very powerful to frame a change. Examples are: Rainbow Nation, Feeding a Hungry Planet, Sustainable Development, Adaptive Stability and Easy Safety. These form a container for new conversations and narratives. The process is shown in Figure 7.5 below.

---

224 Bushe & Marshak, 2018.
225 Bushe, 2019.

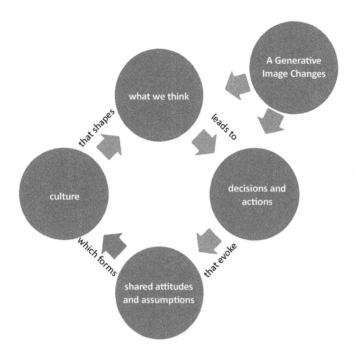

Figure 7.5: How generative images drive change in organisations by changing conversations[226]

CASE STUDY: A FAST GROWING HEALTH CARE ORGANISATION

The Chief Operating Officer of a fast-growing health care organisation, serving a global customer base of patients with a range of difficult to address diseases and afflictions, was concerned about growing problems with poor patient outcomes due to hospital errors. She was well aware of the need to think and act systemically to improve patient safety, but there were plenty of behavioural guidelines in place. She believed the crux of the problem was relationships among the care providers. It was how doctors, nurses and others interacted and communicated that caused the breakdowns that jeopardised care. The medically trained members of the organisation were vertically siloed by their specialties and agreed on very little other than that their specialty needed more money. What patients wanted and needed varied by the nature of

226 Bushe, 2019.

their medical condition and was compounded by different health care practices and cultures in the global communities the organisation sought to serve.

There were also technological and medical innovations coming down the road that needed to be considered, such as the greater use of AI and robots. Unfortunately, the complexity of the situation, wide range of perspectives and lack of agreed upon criteria were compounded by the lack of clear agreement on any system wide changes that might be needed to reduce errors. Attempts to raise the issue tended to result in different groups blaming each other and/or attributing the problems to growth and hiring the wrong people.

Looking for a way to capture the inherent motivation of all the people in the organisation, that would improve relationships across different groups and ultimately result in reduced errors, she challenged everyone in the organisation to propose new initiatives to "Improve our ability to enhance the quality of life of all we serve and touch." A series of Dialogic Organisation Development events that brought together highly diverse groups of people from inside and outside the organisation were run. Some were as short as 90 minutes, a few lasted two days. Each was part of an attempt to launch experiments that people involved were personally committed to.

Surprising things emerged. For example, at a one-day workshop, after examining the strengths and weaknesses of familiar ways of talking about the organisation, its mission, and challenges, one of the participants proposed, "We have to be more like an aqueduct. Strong vertical pillars supporting lateral channels of life-giving substance that flow from us to the people and communities we serve". The participant then drew a rough diagram of an aqueduct. Somehow this "generative image" captured something new and exciting in the participants who began to discuss how their parts of the organisation could be more like an aqueduct. Small groups were encouraged to self-organise around some aspect of the organisation they wanted to change to be more like an aqueduct. One of these groups was composed of different parts of the cardiac unit, and they developed improved communication and coordination (the life-giving flow) processes, but more importantly, developed a shared commitment to working together, that reduced cardiac errors 50% within six months.[227]

☑ Checklist

1. Is your organisation fragile or agile?

2. Do you understand the dominant organisational narrative?

3. Have you moved from diagnostic to dialogic methods?

4. Have you moved from planned to generative change?

5. Are you focusing on both transforming your current organisation and building for the future?

6. Are you proactively building adaptive and resilient cultures?

---

227 Bushe, 2019.

Chapter 8

Redesigning organisations for a new reality

In this chapter, we assess the difficult process of organisation design to challenge current ways of structuring organisations and the need to move to fluid, adaptive, cross-functional teams and fluid resourcing as organising principles. This is one of the most complex processes Human Resources need to work with and well worth our while updating our approach to be future fit.

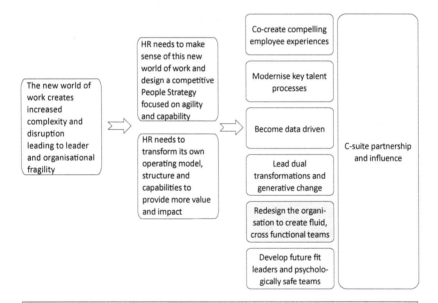

The new world of work creates increased complexity and disruption leading to leader and organisational fragility

HR needs to make sense of this new world of work and design a competitive People Strategy focused on agility and capability

HR needs to transform its own operating model, structure and capabilities to provide more value and impact

Co-create compelling employee experiences

Modernise key talent processes

Become data driven

Lead dual transformations and generative change

Redesign the organisation to create fluid, cross functional teams

Develop future fit leaders and psychologically safe teams

C-suite partnership and influence

Key ideas

- ⊷ Complexity and speed are driving new organisational forms.
- ⊷ Value chain, capability driven organisational designs are more appropriate for a new world of work.
- ⊷ Fluid resource management is critical to get right.
- ⊷ RAPIDs help to steer the process effectively.

Complexity and speed are driving new organisational forms

"A successful organisation is like a colony of bees – a well-structured entity with clear processes and talented contributors who work effectively together."[228]

"Guiding a leader through a significant organisation design project with the goal of building new capabilities may be some of the most important and complex work that a human resource professional can undertake."[229]

"The crisis has forced many to rethink their organizations. Use the opportunity to review your operating model, streamline the organization, reduce duplications and layers, digitize and simplify processes, decrease administration and non-value-added tasks, and to redeploy teams to core activities."[230]

"An organization's design is the arrangement of its components in such a way that it can accomplish the work necessary to effectively and efficiently achieve its business purpose and strategy while delivering high quality customer and employee experience now and into the future."[231]

"Organizational agility – the ability to quickly reconfigure strategy, structure, processes, people, and technology toward value-creating and value-protecting opportunities."[232]

"An adaptive organisation has mechanisms that allows it to shift plans, direction, and resources as needed."[233]

In the past, most organisations were designed for efficiency and effectiveness, leading to complicated and siloed organisations which many organisations have tried to redesign. Galbraith[234] called attention to four

---

228 McKinsey, 2016.
229 Kesler & Kates, 2010.
230 BCG, 2020.
231 LBL strategies, 2020.
232 Salo, 2017.
233 Deshler, 2019.
234 Galbraith, 2012.

---

changes in the business environment that will cause large, hierarchically-structured companies to become too complex:

1. Digitalisation: Big Data could be the next strategic emphasis of future organisations.

2. The move from an economy that is based on mass production that serves mass markets to an economy of mass customisation and segmented markets.

3. The increase in the number and types of stakeholders.

4. The need to take into account market differences across regions and nations.

An addition to these complexities, COVID-19 brought a further set of challenges. To successfully design the organisation of the future, we must first and foremost design less for efficiency and more for speed, agility and adaptability. Efficiency and effectiveness thrive in siloed organisations with clear structures and processes, which are based on predictable commercial patterns. Yet in an era of continuous digital disruption, predictability and structure belong to the past. On the contrary, successful organisations of the future will be the ones that shift away from hierarchical structures to more flexible, team-centric models.[235]

These organisations will facilitate environments that encourage people to meet each other, share knowledge and create project-based teams. Moving from team to team without risks is, and increasingly will be, a critical attribute of the best performing companies. To create an organisation that is future-ready and team-optimised, organisational design must find balance and should be designed through a human-centric approach that creates a sustainable organisational design. This should start with an investment in a crystal-clear future state vision at the onset, which must be relentlessly outcome-driven throughout a co-created experience that honours a healthy team-focused culture.[236]

Organisations of the future will look radically different. Instead of pushing resources and people based on forecasted demand, nimble organisations may instead fluidly enable a broad range of resources and people to be

235 ServiceFutures, 2020.
236 North Highland, 2017.

pulled on an as-needed basis to respond to events in real-time and where they will have the most impact. The organisation needs to be as complex as the business in which it operates and change as fast as its context.

Mercer[237, 238] wrote that vertical hierarchies are being replaced by simpler, more horizontal organisational structures. This change reflects a desire for greater efficiency and lower costs, closer relationships with customers, and increased agility and innovation. We call these new structures heterarchies, as per Figure 8.1 below.

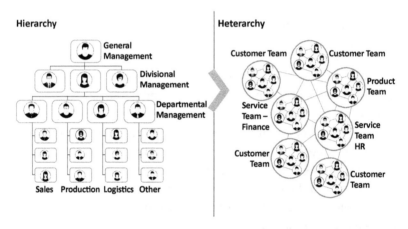

Figure 8.1: From hierarchy to heterarchy (Mercer – project with Roux Consulting)[239]

Cisco, Google and others are already promoting teaming and networking within their organisations. While they have many senior leaders and functional departments, they move people around rapidly, spin up new businesses quickly, and have the ability to start and stop projects at need, moving people into new roles to accommodate changes in priorities.[240]

A flexible structure and the dispersal of decision rights are powerful levers for increasing adaptability. Typically, adaptive companies have replaced permanent silos and functions with modular units that freely communicate and recombine according to the situation at hand. To reinforce this framework, it is helpful to have weak or competing power structures and a

237 Mercer, 2017.

238 Mercer, 2019.

239 Mercer, 2019.

240 Violini et al., 2019.

culture of constructive conflict and dissent. Cisco is one company that has made this transformation. Early on, it relied on a hierarchical, customer-centric organisation to become a leader in the market for network switches and routers. More recently, the CEO, John Chambers, created a novel management structure of cross-functional councils and boards to facilitate moves into developing countries and 30 adjacent and diverse markets (ranging from health care to sports) with greater agility than would previously have been possible.

As they create more-fluid structures, adaptive companies drive decision making down to the front lines, allowing the people most likely to detect changes in the environment to respond quickly and proactively. For example, at Whole Foods the basic organisational unit is the team, and each store has about eight teams. Team leaders – not national buyers – decide what to stock, and they are encouraged to buy from local growers that meet the company's quality and sustainability standards. Teams have veto power over new hires and they are rewarded for their performance; bonuses are based on store profitability over the previous four weeks.

Creating decentralised, fluid, and even competing organisational structures destroys the big advantage of a rigid hierarchy, which is that everyone knows precisely what he or she should be doing. An adaptive organisation cannot expect to succeed unless it provides people with some substitute for that certainty. What is needed is some simple, generative rules to facilitate interaction, help people make trade-offs, and set the boundaries within which they can make decisions.[241]

For a company to stay agile, teams must be formed and disbanded quickly. High-performing companies today may build a "digital customer experience" group, select individuals for the team, and ask them to design and build a new product or service in a year or two. Afterward, the team disperses as team members move on to new projects. This ability to move between teams without risk is a critical attribute of today's high-performing companies.[242]

---

241 Reeves & Deimler, 2011.
242 Deloitte, 2017.

CASE STUDY: LIBERTY MUTUAL INSURANCE

At Liberty Mutual Insurance, teams developing customer-facing products seek to pool talent from different functions, thereby enabling a more agile approach to developing products and onboarding customers. In these efforts, marketing professionals design onboarding collateral, call centre professionals give input on what they are hearing from customers, and finance professionals provide insights into different payment methods. Liberty has found that this teaming leads to improved products, and the team itself feels more empowered. To facilitate this type of teaming across its organisation, Liberty Mutual Insurance has built an entire management system, called the Liberty Management System, to support teams. It specifies how teams are formed, how teams operate, how they measure themselves, and how they communicate with others.[243]

Value chain, capability driven organisational designs are more appropriate for a new world of work

"When faced with an organisation design challenge, many managers rush to grab a cocktail napkin – long the instrument of choice for reorganizing – and sketch out a high-level diagram of boxes and reporting relationships. In doing so, they implicitly accept the way organizational resources and costs are currently deployed and miss opportunities for more creative, effective design. A better course is devoting time to considering what organizational functions truly bring the value proposition to life."[244]

"People shift from fixed individual roles to changing roles, cross-functional expertise, latticed careers and knowing how to activate networks across the organization."[245]

The question is what to base the cross-functional teams and fluid resourcing on. One of the approaches that works is to define the organisation or function value chain and the capabilities (current and future). It is important

---

243 Volini et al., 2019.
244 Beeson, 2014.
245 Deloitte, 2018.

to distinguish between those that the organisation and function owns and those that they need to collaborate or co-create with, as well as to understand what is required to create value for the customer. Critical projects can then be resourced from the capabilities in the value chain. Individuals still belong to a "home", whether it is function or capability or value chain component, but work is delivered in projects and teams. Strong informal relationships and networks ensure optimal collaboration, as is shown in Figure 8.2 below.

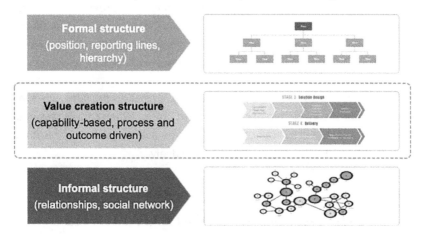

Figure 8.2: Formal, value creation and informal structures[246]

The redesign process follows these steps:

1. Create design principles

Before any work gets underway with re-designing the organisation, clear design principles need to be agreed on. These have to focus on how to create adaptivity and stability in the system in the right balance. Modern design principles recognise that size (large), role clarity (compartmentalisation and levels of authority), specialisation (subdivisions of roles/tasks and tight functionalism) and control are all typical of the traditional type of organisation and are no longer effective. One way to build flexibility into your organisation is to make it one of your design criteria. This encourages leaders to evaluate choices based on whether or not they allow the organisation to flex and adapt.[247]

---

246 Roux Consulting, 2019.
247 Deshler, 2018.

2. Map the value chain and capabilities

Any redesign team should understand the organisational strategy and operating model in depth and map the value creation flow and capabilities accordingly as the base for how work will be done in the future. To create a Value Chain Map, you first need to identify the different "value propositions" (the products or services) that the organisation offers. The value chain describes the different activities that are conducted in order to deliver an end product or service to a customer; an HR function might offer talent development, recruitment, remuneration and organisation development services, while a factory might produce standard products and specials.

The main benefit of the Value Chain Map is that it provides a visual background for considering organisation structure. When capabilities and how work gets delivered are not aligned to the value chain, the organisation cannot deliver its strategy and projects effectively.

CASE STUDY: MARKETING TEAM REDESIGN AROUND VALUE CHAIN AND CAPABILITIES

A retailer decided to merge two functions together to focus on the entire customer experience journey end to end. In order to redesign the function and restructure the ways of working, the below process was followed:

Roux Consulting created a set of design principles, mapped out the value chain and added the capabilities under each component of the value chain. The design principles are shown in Table 8.1 below.

Table 8.1: Client example of design principles

Design principle
Drives strategic outcomes
Builds future capability
Fluid resourcing
Small, independent teams

Design principle
Drives collaboration
Drives speed
Drives innovation and entrepreneurship
Customer driven

The value chain

We used the strategy and customer experience journey maps to map the flow of the value chain for this function. This is shown in Figure 8.3 below. It can be done as a circle or in a linear way.

Our value creation process

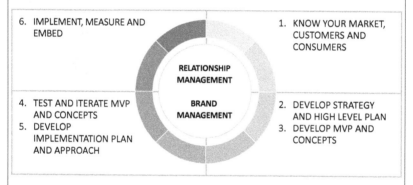

Figure 8.3: The marketing function value chain of a retailer

We then co-created the capabilities that map to this value chain with the team and adjacent teams in the organisation that the team collaborates with. We colour coded the capabilities in terms of which ones reside in the team and which ones they need to collaborate with in other areas. Finally, we tested the Value Chain/Capability Map with the key projects planned for the next 12 months and developed a playbook for the team to use when delivering work. The Value Chain/Capability Map is shown below in Figure 8.4.

Mapping the capabilities and connections

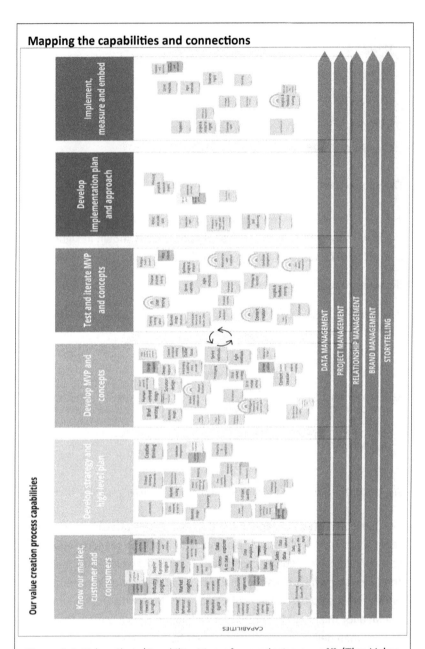

Figure 8.4: Value Chain/Capability Map of a marketing team[248] (The Value Chain/Capability Map is downloadable from: http://www.kr.co.za/ adaptive-hr-value-chain-capability-map

---

248 Roux Consulting, 2019.

Fluid resource management is critical to get right

Once the key projects are agreed on, resources are assigned to them fluidly. In adaptive organisation design, there is often an assumption that people have to be highly fungible and flexible: "Today come in and do this, tomorrow come in and do that; work over here today and over there tomorrow." While there is indeed value and power in that degree of flexibility, most human beings need a degree of stability – a sense of place – to perform at their best. They need to have some degree of certainty around where their place is, what their role is, what they are expected to do, how they can know if they're successful, where to go to get things approved, how to get feedback, and so forth.

CASE STUDY: LARGE ENGINEERING COMPANY

Most of a large engineering company's work is based on projects. Even though the engineers who are assigned to those projects operate very independently, the organisation works well for the most part because an engineer coming back from a project sits on a team of like engineers – for instance a mechanical engineer will sit with other mechanical engineers. They know that when their projects end, they have a place to go – a home base with other mechanical engineers. It may seem minor because most of the work actually happens on the project rather than with the engineering team, but it gives them a sense of place and purpose.[249]

---

249 Deshler, 2019.

CASE STUDY: BEVERAGE COMPANY REDESIGN

A beverage company we worked with opted for a value-creation driven organisational model, combined with key organisational priorities and outcomes, which was governed and coordinated by a PMO-type resourcing and change capability. The employees belonged to a value chain home and delivered their work through cross-functional, 'big bet' projects. This is shown in Figure 8.5 below.

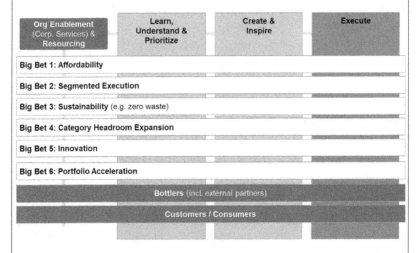

Figure 8.5: A value creation structure where work is delivered through 'big bet' projects.

Key considerations

- Big bets led with lean functional support.

- Work and capability are aligned and focussed on real value creation for all stakeholders, instead of being dissipated across functions.

- Data and technology critical to enable this way of working to ensure value is created. Also dependent on global alignment of functions.

- Fully empowered teams with shared leadership support.

- Metrics, performance enablement and development will evolve significantly.[250]

---

250 Mercer, 2019.

Resource management becomes critical in fluid resourcing designs. A resource manager manages and coordinates the resourcing of projects that are cross-functional in nature (e.g. big bets, new products/services, innovation programmes). These optimise people capability and utilisation to achieve business requirements and individual employee development, and create experiences that lead to enhanced readiness for next roles. Tools like Kimble are very effective in capturing organisational and employee capabilities to facilitate the management of resources.

THE KIMBLE TOOL

The Kimble tool was designed to take administrative tasks away from the resource manager and allow them to focus on providing value added services, which enable their organisations to realise tangible benefits. Kimble allows you to configure your own skills matrix and has comprehensive search functions to help the resource manager match the most appropriate individuals.

It also automatically tracks the actual project assignment experience of the individuals and allows specific project experiences to be captured. This helps find someone not only with the right skills, but also with similar project experience (e.g. industry expertise).

Kimble even allows your consultants and associates/contractors to update their skills profile on a self-serve basis, and has a configurable approval facility for managers to verify these skill levels. Alternatively, the resource manager could look to their associate/ contractor pool for a suitable person. Kimble allows you to store and maintain the skills and availability of an unlimited number of associates/contractors without additional charge and selectively match them against requirements. Figure 8.6 shows the Kimble Resource Analyser tool dashboard.

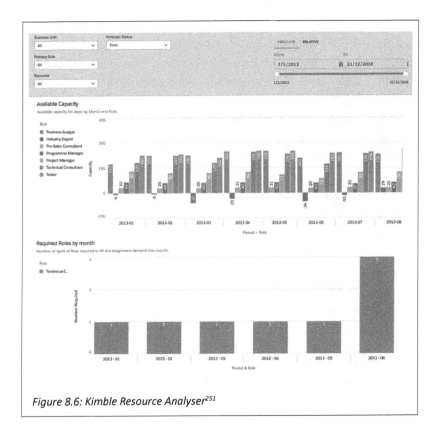

Figure 8.6: Kimble Resource Analyser[251]

RAPIDs help to govern and steer the process effectively

Governance, even more than structure, is one key area that affects the flexibility of an organisation. The first principle in designing an adaptive organisation is that the organisation must have governance mechanisms that allow it to flex and adapt. Mechanisms that allow the company to be governed in a flexible fashion help to override rigid patterns and routines that can slow the organisation's response time and decision making.[252] An example of a RAPID that resources a team across a value chain is shown below in Figure 8.7.

---

251 Kimble, 2020.
252 Deshler, 2019.

RAPID

RAPID: R = Recommend a decision or action, A = Formally agree to a decision, P = Be accountable for performing a decision once made, I = Input, D = Decide (make the decision)

Steps / Roles	Know our market, customers and consumers	Develop strategy and high-level plan	Develop MVP and concepts	Test and iterate MVP and concepts	Develop implementation plan and approach	Implement, measure and embed

Figure 8.7: RAPID across a value chain[253]

---

253 Mercer, 2019.

✎ Checklist

1. How does your organisation design deliver the operating model of the organisation?

2. How does that influence the value chain and capabilities you need?

3. What design principles are we applying when we design our organisation?

4. Are you using cross-functional teams and fluid resourcing?

5. How are you governing the process?

Chapter 9

Leadership and teams 4.0

This chapter covers the need for an updated approach to leadership, leadership development and the leadership of teams in order to successfully deliver the key strategic outcomes and become fast and flexible with high levels of psychological safety and engagement.

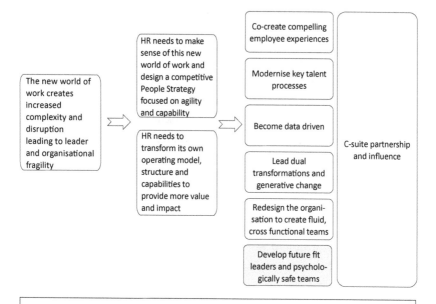

Key ideas

- ↦ Leaders are "in over their heads" and we need to adjust how we define Leadership 4.0.
- ↦ We have to change how we develop leaders.
- ↦ Adaptive, high performing teams are critical for organisational success.
- ↦ Leading virtual teams is the new reality.
- ↦ Psychological safety and diversity are key to high performing teams.

Leaders are "in over their heads" and we need to adjust how we define Leadership 4.0

"The degree to which leaders can manage their own stress and feelings, and the reason why emotional self-awareness and mindfulness are so important in times of crisis, is because leaders become emotional contagions, inflicting positive or negative feelings on others, whether it's family members, friends, colleagues, or subordinates. And, although sometimes leaders may want to induce some stress into a situation to insert new energy and momentum, most of the time it's better to engage people in positive pursuits to retain a higher level of creativity, productiveness, and engagement."[254]

"As a leader in this point in time, you don't want to be faking your emotions. There is an enormous need for genuineness and transparency. And that means some leaders might have to actually train themselves to be caring, curious, and positive, which is hard to do when you're in a state of threat or fear, when self-protection becomes an overwhelming instinct. There is a strong temptation to just dive right in to business without acknowledging what others might be up against. Best practice is therefore to stop, pause, breathe, and remind yourself to be genuinely interested in what's going on for others."[255]

Leadership and how leaders are developed has changed significantly in the context of the future of work, and traditional leadership development criteria and models are limited in their ability to address these changes. This has resulted in leaders struggling to deal with the pace and complexity of their context and feeling exposed and vulnerable. Practitioners, on the other hand, are currently faced with a complexity of approaches and models to choose from, and no real starting point for developing leaders for the future of work context.

Leadership scholars have certainly noted this significant increase in the challenges that leaders face in the new world of work 4.0. The question is whether our thinking as scholars and practitioners has significantly evolved to ensure that we present models and practices of leadership that truly

---

254 Boyatzis, 2020 (in De Semet & Schaninger, 2020).

255 Edmondson, 2020 (in DeSmet and Schaninger, 2020). It is an interview with Boyatizis and Edmondson conducted by DeSmet and Schaninger for the McKinsey Quarterly, July 2020.

address the complexity leaders face? It seems not – we are spending more and more on developing leaders with whom employees are less and less satisfied. A CEC European Mangers report[256] noted that despite, or even partly due to, a growing leadership industry with an estimated $130 – $356 billion spent per year on leadership development alone, there seems to be a profound conceptual confusion about what leadership is. In fact, only 10% of leaders are at the level required to deal with the complexity and disruption of our current context, and the gap grows larger the more senior leaders become (see Figure 9.1 below).

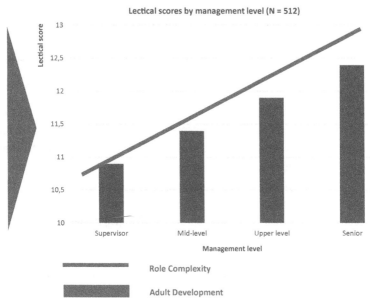

Lectical scores by management level (N = 512)

Developmental Score	Percentage in Population	Cynefin Framework	Contextual Thinking	Solutions
Advanced linear thinking (10.5 – 10.9)	60%	Can work with *simple* problems	Considers the people involved as causes	Weighs perspectives against one another, then chooses one
Early systems thinking (11.0 – 11.4)	30%	Can work with *complicated* problems	Considers the immediate context as a cause	Gathers information from stakeholders, then attempts to build a solution that gives all stakeholders something they want

256 CEC, 2017.

Developmental Score	Percentage in Population	Cynefin Framework	Contextual Thinking	Solutions
Advanced systems thinking (11.5 – 11.9)	9%	Can work with *complex* problems	Considers the broader context as a cause including systems and culture	Identifies and leverages one or more broad interests that are common to all stakeholders
Early principled thinking (12.0 – 12.4)	1%	Can work with *chaotic* problems	Identifies "root" or systemic causes that shape the contexts Works with others to design systemic solutions	Identifies solutions for dissolving common polarities (e.g., the good of employee vs. organization)

Figure 9.1: The Leadership Complexity Gap[257]

COVID-19 has made the need for developing leaders more urgent than ever before. Companies are going through times of turbulence and need to reimagine themselves, innovate business models and accelerate their digital transformation. Leaders need to support the emotional health of people, demonstrate and communicate hope and opportunity, ensure that their teams are motivated and engaged, and perform at their best. They themselves need to remain grounded and deliberately calm while making wise decisions under pressure and stress.[258]

Veldsman and Johnson described the dilemma we find ourselves in:[259]

"Leadership is in an overheating crucible of a reframed world in the throes of fundamental and radical transformation. The search is on for better and different leadership. Without any doubt leadership is the critical strategic capability of nations, communities and organisations, making them sustainably future-fit. To the best of our knowledge, no overall, systemic, integrated and holistic view of leadership exists, and few organisations adopt a systemic, integrated approach to leadership."

This is partly because, despite the evolution of leadership and organisations, scholars and practitioners still seem to prefer to focus on standardised,

---

257 Lectical, 2015.
258 Van Dam & Coates, 2020.
259 Veldsman & Johnson, 2016, p. 1-2.

predictable and observable approaches like competence, traits and behaviours rather than the more difficult, nebulous factors of mindset, ethics and adult development. Oversimplified and fixed models of leadership do not acknowledge the inherent complexity of human behaviour and the context within which this behaviour occurs.[260] Pick up any of the popular books on leadership today and you will still find a list of traits that are thought to be central to effective leadership. The main problem with using traits as a dominant approach is that it negates adult development and neuroplasticity research that believes people can develop further as leaders by supposing leaders are born with innate traits. The approach fixes the effectiveness of leadership and limits the value of learning and teaching in regard to leadership. Innate personality traits may indeed not be as fixed or influential in leadership as the theory proposes.

A WEF report calls for new leadership capabilities for the 4IR[261], arguing that, "The traditional leadership model of central control no longer fits. The skill sets required by leaders to manage the new organisation have vastly changed. In today's complex work environment, leaders should lead with purpose and ensure the use of the tools of technology, culture, processes and structure".

In 2018/2019, I interviewed 22 thought leaders in the field to understand what their key challenges were and mapped their responses in a word cloud (see Figure 9.2). The key themes that emerged were mainly related to the complexity they are facing in increasingly changing environments, contexts, organisations, work and world. Furthermore, these challenges are global. It became clear that the respondents believed leaders were struggling as more was being asked from them. Other themes relate to some of the challenges themselves, namely the dynamic and ambiguous nature of the challenges and growing expectations, the public nature of everything they do, the level of transformation required of them and their organisations, the level of ongoing development required to stay relevant, the impact of AI and digital, and the amount of adaptive problems/agile approaches they have to deal with which feel at times unrealistic. The consequences of leaders feeling overwhelmed seem to manifest in toxic behaviours, the seduction of power, feelings of being isolated, and a narrow focus on technical problems. There

---

260 Singh, 2014.
261 WEF, 2019.

is thus a growing call for a more human- and people-centred approach, and for leaders to work on their identity as part of this.

Figure 9.2: Leadership challenges from 22 interviews with thought leaders[262]

Gloor[263] and Kelly[264] described Leadership 4.0 as Swarm Leadership, i.e. leadership that is adaptive, emergent, connected, responsive and collaborative. They saw it as forming part of the collective theories of leadership, but pointed out how it differs from shared and distributed leadership by being part of a self-organising, complex, adaptive system. They described this type of leadership as responsive – leaders responding to situations in an intentionally adaptive way. As leaders increasingly lead from the side, they become the orchestrator of the fluid workforce, bringing together the right skills, talent and experiences to create value. Developing leadership capabilities in the current context will require that HR leaders move from their traditional model of leadership that is reactive and based on command and control, to a purpose- and values-driven model of leadership that is adaptive, agile, and focused on building the organisational culture and empowering the workforce of the future.

Leadership 4.0 is integrative, complex and multi-layered. There is a need for lifelong horizontal and vertical development journeys using adult

---

262 Roux, 2020.
263 Gloor, 2017.
264 Kelly, 2019.

development theory, virtuous cycles and neuroplasticity as core theories of continuous growth. Leadership needs to be scaled to enable work in new contexts of digital, virtual and flexible environments that are in constant flux, with wicked problems that can only be solved collectively. In my PhD research, I found the following evolutionary themes of leadership:

Leadership 1.0	Leadership 2.0 and 3.0	Leadership 4.0
		Integrative
		Holistic, deep
		Eco systemic
	Visionary	Lifelong
Hero leadership	Charismatic	Complex
Trait theory	Transformational	Neuro plasticity
Command and control	Behavioural	Horizontal and vertical
Competencies	Conceptual redundancy	Agile and adaptive
Job security	Horizontal	Broad roles
Hierarchy	Competencies	Scaling leadership
Narrow tasks and roles	Empowerment	Digital
Office bound	Culture	Turbulent
Traditional	Modern	Technology
Socialised	Socialised	Virtual and flexible
	Situational	Self management
		Post-modern
		Self authoring
		Journeys

Figure 9.3: Roux PHD research (2019 in Maturing Leadership).[265]

There are some great examples of these kind of leaders emerging in the world. I share a few of them in the following case studies.

CASE STUDY: GRAVITY CEO DAN PRICE

The impact of COVID-19 was devastating for Gravity. A Seattle-based company, Gravity Payments helped small businesses around the US to process payments, but as those businesses took a nosedive, so did Gravity. The CEO, Dan Price, was facing a crushing decision – cut 20% of his people or go bankrupt. Then, he had a brilliant idea: ask employees for help.

On March 19, Price called a companywide meeting to let employees know the state of the business and solicit creative strategies for

265 Roux, 2019 (Leadership 4.0, Chapter 1 in Maturing Leadership – edited by Jonathan Reams, Emerald Publishers).

navigating the next few months. He and Gravity COO Tammi Kroll also scheduled 40 hour-long meetings with small groups of employees to check in and gather ideas. "We just put all our cards on the table", Price says. "And we listened."

Price, who had made headlines in the past when he took a pay cut to increase his employees' minimum salary to $70,000, decided to take the problem to his people. Everyone was willing to make a sacrifice, but not everyone could afford to give up the same amount. Each person was then given a form that allowed them to privately express what they could or could not sacrifice. Price was hailed for his empathy, transparency and emotional intelligence.[266]

CASE STUDY: UNILEVER'S PAUL POLMAN

Paul Polman's decade-long tenure as Unilever CEO redefined the meaning of good business. From his first day in 2009, he set ambitious goals for the now-$57 billion maker of household goods that put purpose on a par with profit. That meant multi-stakeholder capitalism, in which focusing on the interests of employees, suppliers, retailers and the environment would ultimately benefit investors, and the Unilever Sustainable Living Plan (USLP), a set of commitments based on the United Nations' Sustainable Development Goals (SDGs), to improve social impact in tandem with boosting sales. During his tenure, Unilever outperformed its industry on both the top and bottom lines, and delivered an impressive 290% shareholder return.

"For me, sustainable development is first and foremost about inclusion and living in harmony with planet Earth. Human health and planetary health go hand in hand, as the recent COVID virus reminds us once more. When you fight for equal opportunity for everybody, for example, for people to have access to education or food or clean drinking water, you fight for basic human values, which are the bedrock of functioning societies – dignity and respect, equity and compassion. Any time you violate that, as we've seen so often in the past 20 or 30 years, people suffer. It makes us all responsible. If you know that climate change kills

---

266 Bariso, 2020.

eight million people a year, and you then continue to be a contributor to climate change, you are complicit. If 826 million people still go to bed hungry and you waste food, you are also part of the issue. If you continue to buy from irresponsible companies that encourage slave labour or pay less than fair wages, you are equally irresponsible.

There are some of these human values that I think we're given very early in our lives. I'm very grateful for my parents; they really had these broader values. Partly as a result of my religious upbringing as well, I've always felt that our duty here in this world is to serve others and simply make it a better place than we found it. Obviously we need all the basic skills required to run a company. But I always say, "A good leader is first and foremost a good human being." That's a very important part. And the second is being purpose-driven. You need to discover your purpose because it's that purpose that gives you energy. Hopefully the company purpose reinforces yours and you help reinforce the company's. It's a symbiosis that makes you feel at home and helps you be successful. Also key is to create an environment where each and every one can develop to his or her fullest potential."[267]

Through my research, I developed a multi-layered model of Leadership 4.0 that captures the need for core leadership mindsets like growth mindset, curiosity and learning agility as a core requirement for leaders in the new world of work. It also highlights the importance of seeing leadership in context and as part of an eco-system guided by levels of work. This model rests on a foundation of ethical and moral maturity, which is enabled though adult and ego development, intentional behaviours and updated adaptive competencies. This flips the trait and competency theories on their heads. The model is shown below in Figure 9.4.

---

267 Reynolds, 2020.

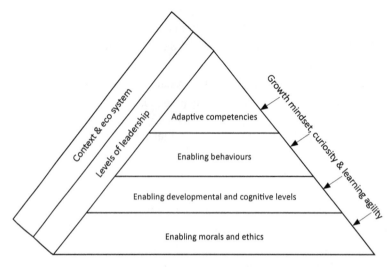

Figure 9.4: A model of leadership 4.0

We have to change how we develop leaders

"Over 90% of current leadership development is not fit for purpose."[268]

"The leadership industry has not in any major, meaningful, measurable way improved the human condition."[269]

The new context therefore puts leadership development in the spotlight as there is an increased urgency to develop leaders in a way that is impactful and relevant. There are, however, several constraints in doing so, including diverse perspectives, disparate research and practice, old methods and pedagogies, and disconnected development. De Smet et al.[270] described the more recent challenges as accelerating the need for leaders that can bring people together, energise them forward, and reimagine the new normal. A new approach is urgently needed in leadership development interventions. It needs to be non-linear, an exercise in critical thinking and problem-solving, aid one's sense making capabilities that can be communicated to the collective, as well as extend roles and responsibilities that are more distributed among followers. New leadership development programmes need to refocus efforts from developing skill sets to developing mindsets.

268 Hawkins, 2018.
269 Kellerman, 2018 (in Hawkins, 2018).
270 De Smet et al., 2020.

We simply cannot continue to spend the amounts of money we do on leadership development and continue to see trust in leaders falling.

Veldsman stated it thus:

"Currently, the spontaneous kneejerk response to address the growing need for better and different leadership, as well as to deal with the deepening, widening leadership crisis, is to embark on a frenetic search for THE silver bullet to resolve the crisis. E.g., the search for a specific or different ability/quality, e.g. resilience; a particular intelligence, e.g. emotional or cultural intelligence; a certain level of maturity; intense ethical training, in combination with more stringent ethical codes and governance; or a single ingredient of authentic leadership like greater self-insight, genuine relationships. This response manifests a future-unfit vantage point in viewing leadership from a short term, individualistic, simplistic, narrow, fragmented and shallow perspective."[271]

According to my PhD research, the clear themes that need to be incorporated into leadership development approaches in the new world of work are:

- development based on adult and vertical development;
- a focus on collective AND individual development;
- embedded in context and messy reality;
- transformative, constructive learning pedagogy used – immersion, experience, reflection and practice;
- co-designed lifelong learning journeys that are evaluated, tracked and adjusted in real-time; and
- a blended and digital approach.[272]

The leadership development model I propose is shown below in Figure 9.5.

---

271 Veldsman & Johnson, 2016, p. 4.
272 Roux, 2020.

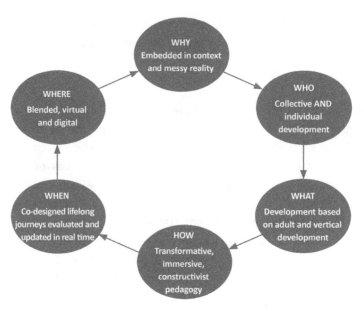

Figure 9.5: Proposed leadership development model fit for the future of work and post COVID context[273]

Using a simplified and integrated leadership development model, with key leadership development criteria fit for the future of work, is a starting point for the assessment and design of the fit for leadership development programme and interventions for the context of the future of work. It avoids the pitfalls of traditional approaches and leverages the emerging practices triangulated in the literature and in practice.

Organisations like Novartis have completely updated how they see leadership and how they develop it across their organisations with great success.

CASE STUDY: NOVARTIS

unbossed

Our approach to empowering our people is inspired by ideas explored in the book "UNBOSS" by Lars Kolind and Jacob Bøtter. In 2019, 350 senior leaders began a yearlong leadership development programme to build the capabilities they need to help transform our culture. So far, 120 have completed it, with the rest due to finish in 2020.

273 Roux, 2020.

Members of the Executive Committee of Novartis (ECN) are going through the same intensive program, which includes a two-week immersion session supported by coaching, as well as webinars, and three 360-degree evaluations to track progress. We plan to cascade key aspects of the programme to 10 000 leaders over the next three years, helping embed the new leadership approach in our organization.

NOVARTIS CEO VASANT NARASIMHAN

"Unbossing" companies by reinventing outdated management hierarchies is the key to leadership success, according to one chief executive. Speaking at the One Young World conference, Vasant Narasimhan, CEO of pharmaceutical giant Novartis, described himself as an "accidental CEO," and emphasized that leadership still carried huge importance.

"The most powerful thing we have that can improve the world is leadership," he said. "The most precious resource we have is leadership. The reason society has been able to make so many extraordinary gains over the last century is leadership."

Narasimhan also urged future leaders to stay grounded as they were given more responsibility and authority. "Leadership is not a right, it's not a rank – it's something that you earn every single day," he said. However, Narasimhan said traditional attitudes toward management were from a bygone era and needed an overhaul.

He said the corporate world was slowly learning the "wisdom of ancient (societies)," noting that many big firms were built during a different time and had been slow to adapt to a changing workforce. "Along the way we lost that," he said. "Somewhere in the last 100 years we've moved to a world of knowledge workers. We can't manage those workers like cogs in a factory."

He told the conference that Novartis was on a journey to "unboss" itself and become less hierarchical. "The source of power for a leader is your ability to create opportunities for the people around you," he explained.

"People have to follow you because they believe in your ideas and your values. If the reason you want to do something is to please the hierarchy (you risk losing that)."

The company's "unbossing" movement aims to develop "servant leaders who put their teams' success above their own," a spokesperson for Novartis told CNBC via email on Tuesday. This has involved investing in several projects, including a leadership programme for Novartis' top 300 leaders, which has been dubbed the "Unbossed Leadership Experience."

Narasimhan himself, as well as the company's executive committee, are among the participants in the year-long leadership development program, which involves webinars, simulations, social learning and personalized coaching designed to train leaders in delivering the "unbossed" culture. Novartis is also using specially-developed online surveys to give employee feedback to managers. The platform was initially used for the firm's top 350 leaders but is now in the process of being rolled out to all 12,000 managers across the company.[274]

Adaptive, high performing teams are critical for organisational success

"In our research with high-performing teams, we've asked clients to reflect on their 'peak experiences,' and many, particularly energy companies, would almost always reflect on coming back from natural disasters. Many describe a period when all hands are on deck, bureaucracy is stripped away, and the teams unite around a moral higher calling."[275]

Teams are becoming more complex – cross disciplined, global, project-based, technology-enabled and structured around the customer, with people shifting in and out of teams more regularly. The original conceptualisation of teams considered them to be intact, tightly bounded, and coupled with members from a single organisation who are co-located, interacting face-to-face to generate an identifiable product, service or solution. Conversely, teams today consist of members from multiple organisations shifting in and out of teams while relying heavily on technology to complete a

---

274 Taylor, 2019.
275 Schaninger, 2020 (in DeSmet and Schaninger).

variety of tasks. HR leaders need to understand the new world of teams – virtual, diverse, cross-functional – and help leaders to facilitate inclusion, psychological safety and high performance.

Flat hierarchies, close-knit working environments, open workspaces and virtual teams – this is what the modern business world is about. Small, independent teams are the lifeblood of the agile organisation. Top executives can unleash them by driving ambition, removing red tape, and helping managers adjust to the new norms. "Virtual" teams – ones made up of people in different physical locations – are on the rise. As companies expand geographically and as telecommuting becomes more common, work groups often span far-flung offices, shared workspaces, private homes and hotel rooms. Yet whether physical or virtual, local or global, the enabling conditions of teams remain the same:

1. Compelling direction: the foundation of every great team is a direction that energises, orients and engages its members. Teams cannot be inspired if they don't know what they're working toward and don't have explicit goals. Those goals should be challenging (modest ones don't motivate) but not so difficult that the team becomes dispirited. They also must be consequential.

2. Strong structure: teams need the right mix and number of members, optimally designed tasks and processes, and norms that discourage destructive behaviour and promote positive dynamics. High-performing teams include members with a balance of skills; every individual doesn't have to possess superlative technical and social skills, but the team overall needs a healthy dose of both. Diversity in knowledge, views and perspectives, as well as in age, gender and race, can help teams be more creative and avoid groupthink.

3. Supportive context: having the right support is the third condition that enables team effectiveness. This includes maintaining a reward system that reinforces good performance, an information system that provides access to the data needed for the work, an educational system that offers training, and last – but not least – securing the material resources required to do the job, such as funding and technological assistance. While no team ever gets everything it wants, leaders can head off a lot of problems by taking the time to get the essential pieces in place from the start.

4. Shared mindset: establishing the first three enabling conditions will pave the way for team success, as Hackman and his colleagues showed, but our research indicates that today's teams need something more. Distance and diversity, as well as digital communication and changing membership, make them especially prone to the problems of "us versus them" thinking and incomplete information. The solution to both is developing a shared mindset among team members – something team leaders can do by fostering a common identity and common understanding.[276]

CASE STUDY: GOOGLE

Google reviewed over 180 Google teams, conducting more than 200 interviews, analysing 250-plus attributes they identified, and cross-comparing the makeup of stellar groups and those that weren't reaching such heights, and found five key dynamics of successful teams. While all five play a role, the first trait, psychological safety, was substantially more crucial to overall success. As Google put it, psychological safety is based on a primary question: "Can we take risks on this team without feeling insecure or embarrassed?"

Figure 9.6 shows the five key dynamics that set successful teams apart, according to Google research.

Figure 9.6: What makes a Google team effective?[277]

276 Haas & Mortensen, 2016.
277 Kim, 2017.

TOOL: DOES YOUR TEAM MEASURE UP?

Based on a *Harvard Business Review* article, Figure 9.7 provides us with a tool to look at team effectiveness.

Does Your Team Measure Up?

To see how your team is doing, evaluate it on the three classic criteria of team effectiveness. Then look at how ell it meets the four conditions that drive the success of teams in a diverse, dispersed, digital, dynamic business. Under performance on the criteria and weaknesses in the conditions are usually linked. Understanding the connections between them can help your team identify ways to improve.

On a scale of 1 (worst) to 5 (best), rate your team on these criteria:

OUTPUT	COLLABORATIVE ABILITY	INDIVIDUAL DEVELOPMENT
Are our customers happy with our output – with its quality, quantity, and delivery?	Do our team's dynamics help us work well together?	Are individual team members improving their knowledge, skills, and abilities?

Then score your team on the following aspects of the conditions for effectiveness:

COMPELLING DIRECTION	STRONG STRUCTURE	SUPPORTIVE CONTEXT	SHARED MINDSET
Do we have a common goal that is clear, challenging (but not impossible), and consequential?	Do we have the right number and mix of members?	Do we have the resources, information, and training we need?	Do the team members have a strong common identity?
	Are people responsible for tasks from beginning to end?	Are there appropriate rewards for success?	Do we readily share information with one another and understand one another's constraints and context?
	Do we have clear norms for acceptable conduct?		

This assessment draws on the seminal research of the organizational-behavior expert J. Richard Hackman. You can find more of his insights in *Leading Teams: Setting the Stage for Great Performance* (Harvard Business School Publishing, 2002).

Figure 9.7: Team Measurement Tool[278]

---

278 Haas & Mortensen, 2016.

TOOL: TEAM CHARTER CANVAS

Once you understand the issues your team faces, you can use a Team Charter Canvas to agree a framework that guides the team. A great example is shown below in Figure 9.8.

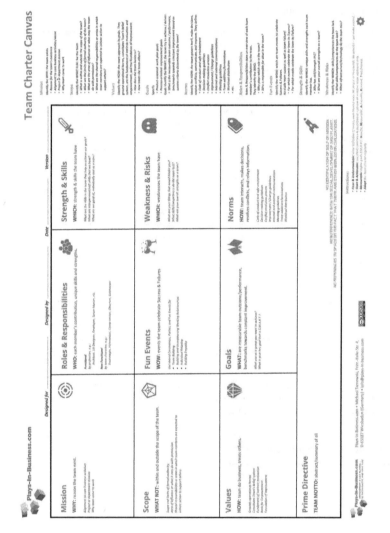

Figure 9.8: Team Charter Canvas[279] (Download this poster from: https://www.plays-in-business.com/download/team-charter-canvas-poster-a0-format/)

---

279 Team Charter Canvas, 2020.

Leading virtual teams is the new reality

When building a remote team, you'll need to rethink all processes, from recruiting to onboarding, career paths, performance reviews, collaboration, tools and project management.

When setting up virtual teams, start by asking these questions:

- What kinds of information do you need to share?

- Do you need to work on documents together? Do you need a way to share tasks or calendars? Do you need to document decisions in wikis?

- Where is this information stored?

- How will you communicate with each other?

- How will you know what projects or assignments are being worked on?

- Do you need to set core hours or can the work be done asynchronously?

- How will you give each other feedback?

- How will we learn more about each other?[280]

TOOL: REMOTE TEAM CULTURE CANVAS[281]

As most organisations are going remote, trust issues are surfacing; productivity is suffering, people are overwhelmed, and most teams have lost their rhythm. Few organisations were prepared to embrace remote work, which requires more trust, freedom and flexibility than usual. Organisations cannot expect people to work the same way but via Zoom; teams must define norms for how they're going to meet and interact.

How can you keep your culture strong when everyone is working from home? You have to remote-proof your culture. The Remote Culture Canvas, a simplified version of the Culture Design Canvas, will help you structure that conversation. An example is shown in Figure 9.9 below.

---

280 Redbooth, 2020.
281 Razzetti, 2020.

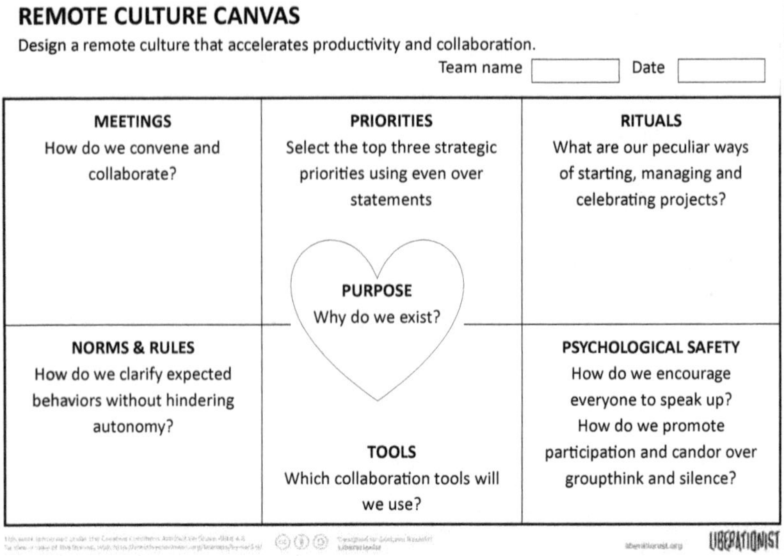

REMOTE CULTURE CANVAS

Design a remote culture that accelerates productivity and collaboration.

Team name [   ]   Date [   ]

MEETINGS	PRIORITIES	RITUALS
How do we convene and collaborate?	Select the top three strategic priorities using even over statements	What are our peculiar ways of starting, managing and celebrating projects?

PURPOSE
Why do we exist?

NORMS & RULES		PSYCHOLOGICAL SAFETY
How do we clarify expected behaviors without hindering autonomy?	**TOOLS** Which collaboration tools will we use?	How do we encourage everyone to speak up? How do we promote participation and candor over groupthink and silence?

Figure 9.9: Remote Culture Canvas for teams

Create a draft version of the canvas, writing big ideas on large Post-it notes. Think of this as your first prototype – don't overthink it. Each participant should do this on their own before they start working together.[282]

Psychological safety and diversity are key to high performing teams

Research shows that the most successful teams are cognitively diverse and psychologically safe. Diverse teams make better decisions up to 87% of the time IF there is psychological safety in the team.

---

282 Razzetti, 2020.

CASE STUDY: DIVERSE TEAMS FOCUS MORE ON THE FACTS AND PROCESS FACTS MORE CAREFULLY

People from diverse backgrounds might actually alter the behaviour of a group's social majority in ways that lead to improved and more accurate group thinking. In a study published in the *Journal of Personality and Social Psychology*, scientists assigned 200 people to six-person mock jury panels whose members were either all white or included four white and two black participants. The people were shown a video of a trial of a black defendant and white victims. They then had to decide whether the defendant was guilty.

It turned out that the diverse panels raised more facts related to the case than homogenous panels, and made fewer factual errors while discussing available evidence. If errors did occur, they were more likely to be corrected during deliberation. One possible reason for this difference was that white jurors on diverse panels recalled evidence more accurately than jurors on all white panels.[283]

Amy Edmondson and Timothy Clarke have developed great tools to help us nurture more psychologically safe teams and workplaces. Clarke developed a 4-stage model that helps to grow psychological safety one step at a time in a team. This model is shown below in Figure 9.10.

---

283 Rock & Grant, 2016.

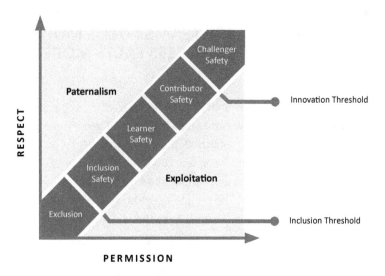

Figure 9.10: The four quadrants of psychological safety[284]

According to Laura Delizonna, here is how one should develop psychological safety:[285]

1. Approach conflict as a collaborator, not an adversary.

2. Speak human to human.

3. Anticipate reactions and plan countermoves.

4. Replace blame with curiosity.

5. Ask for feedback on delivery.

6. Measure psychological safety.

TOOL: PSYCHOLOGICAL SAFETY TEAM SURVEY

Another great tool to use with a team is to assess their level of psychological safety. Amy Edmondson provided a useful questionnaire, as seen in Figure 9.11 below.

---

284 Clark, 2020.

285 Delizonna, 2017.

Psychological Safety: Team Survey

On great teams, people feel psychologically safe, they feel comfortable speaking up, asking questions, and admitting mistakes. To help us better understand our own team's climate for psychological safety, please complete this survey.

Rate the following statements on a scale from 1 (Strongly Disagree) to 5 (Strongly Agree):

		Strongly Disagree				Strongly Agree
		1	2	3	4	5
	Part 1: Individual Safety					
1	In this team it is easy to discuss difficult issues and problems.					
2	I won't receive retaliation or criticism if I admit an error or mistake.					
3	It is easy to ask members of this team for help.					
4	I feel safe offering new ideas, even if they aren't fully-formed plans.					
	Part 2: Team Respect					
5	In this team, people are accepted for being different.					
6	My teammates welcome my ideas and give them time and attention.					
7	Members of this team could easily describe the value of each others' contributions.					
	Part 3: Team Learning					
8	On this team, people talk about mistakes and ways to prevent and learn from them.					
9	We take time to find new ways to improve our team's work processes.					
10	Members of this team raise concerns they have about team plans or decisions.					
11	We try to discover our underlying assumptions and seek counterarguments about issues under discussion.					

Figure 9.11: Psychological safety[286]

---

286 Edmondson, 1999.

✎ Checklist

1. Is your view of leadership 1.0, 2.0, 3.0 or 4.0?

2. Is your leadership development "fit for purpose"?

3. Is there an intentional effort to enable teams and build psychological safety?

4. How diverse are your teams?

5. Have you remote-proofed your teams?

CHAPTER 10

Bringing it all together

In this chapter, we talk about where to start the journey and how to get the ear and support of the Board and the C-suite in order to drive the successful transformation of HR and of the organisation in the process. Earning credibility and building strong partnerships with business leaders are critical to shifting an organisation's thinking about HR.

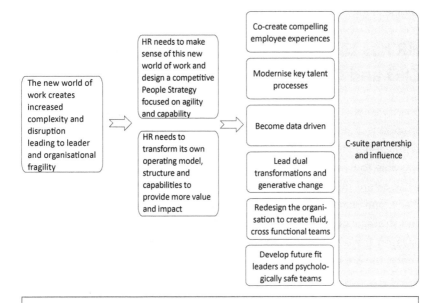

Key ideas

- HR has to work in a powerful alliance with the CEO and CFO.
- You have to report your key outcomes and tell powerful stories.

"The fourth industrial revolution and its repercussions for the future of work offer the HR profession a unique opportunity to redefine its mission and advance its function. HR can achieve this by becoming, beyond employment, the referent of work as a whole, while guaranteeing the qualification of the workforce through the creation of a culture of continuous learning and skills assessment."[287]

"As the fourth industrial revolution transforms work and the workforce, HR professionals must respond to proactively manage the future of work. Human resources managers will increasingly have to develop their skills and understanding in data and technology analysis, and help employees develop these skills in order to enhance their experience and encourage their productivity."[288]

"Companies should be flexible with their human capital, and CHROs should recommend actions that will unlock or create value. The reassignment of people along with capital reallocation is what really boosts companies."[289]

HR has to work in a powerful alliance with the CEO and CFO

Charan et al.[290] wrote that CEOs do not yet rate HR as one of the most important functions of their companies. In 2016, KPMG International conducted a study on HR and found that only 17% of respondents felt HR was able to demonstrate its value to the business in a measurable way. To what extent do you and your team influence the priorities set, decisions made, and actions taken by leaders in pursuit of your organisation's vision and strategic objectives? Are you satisfied with the impact you are able to have on the way your organisation goes about leveraging the talent and energy of your work force?

While ultimately it is the CEO or business owner who must mandate the role that HR gets to play, a skilled and influential HR leader can shift an organisation's thinking and improve the strength of their team's ability to influence. Among the most important ways to strengthen your team's position are to earn credibility and build strong partnerships with business leaders.[291] With COVID-19 this has created a flipped scenario where HR has

---

287 Jesuthasan, 2020 (in Fanning, 2020).
288 Zahidi, 2020 (in Fanning, 2020).
289 Charan et al., 2015.
290 Charan et al., 2015.
291 Gately, 2015.

had to lead the emergency response.[292] During this time of major upheaval and uncertainty, the CHRO is a loud voice in the coronavirus corporate war room who is busy helping CEOs oversee their remote workforces and developing return-to-work plans for when the economy reboots.

These Chief People Officers are the ones having daily, if not hourly, conversations with their CEOs and other senior leaders on how best to navigate a situation that no one could possibly have fathomed. They're the ones helping to keep anxiety-ridden employees informed about what's happening with the company, as well as up-to-date on the resources – financial and medical – that can help them stay calm and productive. And as organisations begin discussions about when employees might be able to return to work, it's the CHRO's job to help create a blueprint for what that might look like.

Coronavirus has elevated the role of HR Chiefs in the C-suite; this is a moment to leverage. HR has to take up its strategic role next to the Finance function and together form a powerful triad with the CEO to drive the organisational change required to survive in a fast changing, disruptive world. It is up to the CEO to elevate HR and address barriers that prevent HR from becoming a strategic partner.

At Verizon, for example, since March 11, CEO Hans Vestberg and CHRO Christy Pambianchi have led a daily all-hands for the company's 135,000 employees. At Accenture, Chief Leadership and Human Resources Officer Ellyn Shook now meets virtually with company leaders twice a week – instead of in-person once a quarter – to discuss key people and operations issues. And at Cisco, Chief People Officer Fran Katsoudas is leading, along with CEO Chuck Robbins, a weekly meeting for all 75,900 employees. This meeting, which used to be monthly, is an example, as she told me, of how "the workplace is becoming the new definition of community.... Sometimes our employees bring in their families. We talk about business updates. We talk about mental health and wellbeing. We laugh a little about seeing each other's homes, kids, and pets on WebEx." It is CHROs who are stepping up to create agile cultures, not only responding to employee needs but seeing around the corner – giving permission and support, and role modelling empathy, compassion and inclusive leadership.[293]

---

292 Caminiti, 2020.
293 Huffington, 2020.

The ability of HR to anticipate change and make sense of the varying environment for the Board and the rest of the C-suite is a game changer when it comes to the ability to influence more effectively. It comes down to using data and analytics and a combination of contextual intelligence and sense making skills.[294] DDI's Global Leadership Forecast 2018 found that HR professionals who are succeeding with analytics are 6.3 times more likely to get opportunities for advancement than those who aren't, and 3.6 times more liable to have a strong reputation with senior business leaders. The credibility you earn and strength of partnership you are able to build determine the influence you will have on the performance of your business.

Another emerging leverage point for HR impact is the increasing focus of culture, talent, capability and wellness issues at a Board level. Ben Lawrence, Chief Human Resource Officer of Wesfarmers in Australia, noted that: "I've seen a real change in my time in senior HR roles, both in terms of the conversations with boards and the frequency of the conversations." Lawrence and his HR team have a minimum of one or two formal sessions a year with the Wesfarmers Board, discussing talent management, succession, diversity, as well as the depth and quality of leadership.[295]

CASE STUDY: MARSH

CEO Peter Zaffino often has one-on-one discussions with his CFO, Courtney Leimkuhler, and his CHRO, Mary Anne Elliott. In April 2015 he held a meeting with both of them to assess the alignment of the organisation with desired business outcomes. The three of them began their meeting by selecting a business in the portfolio and drawing a vertical line down the middle of a blank page on a flip chart. The right side was for business performance (Leimkuhler's expertise) and the left side for organisational design issues (Elliott's expertise). A horizontal line created boxes for the answers to two simple questions: What is going well? What is not going well?

---

294 Lee & Wilkie, 2018.
295 Donaldson, 2013.

Working together to synthesise disparate data points into one flip chart helped the team to identify items on the organisational side that would predict business performance in the next four to eight quarters. Significant value came from the dialogue as connections emerged naturally. Zaffino commented that:

"We constantly drill down deep to understand why a business is performing the way it is. In those instances, we are drilling vertically, not horizontally, when there could be some items identified on the organizational side that are actually driving the performance." Zaffino cited the implementation of a new sales plan, which HR was working on, as one example. His concern was making sure business results were aligned with remuneration "so we didn't have sales compensation becoming disconnected from the overall financial result of the business. We also didn't want to drive top-line growth without knowing how to invest back in the business and increase profitability". The CHRO was thinking it through from her perspective: Is this sales plan motivating the right behaviours so that it moves business performance to the "going well" category?

Seeing the interconnections also helped the trio identify what mattered most. "It's easy enough to list everything we want to do better", Leimkuhler said, "but it's hard to know where to start. When you understand which things on the organizational side are really advancing business performance, it makes it easier to prioritize". For example, managing the transition of regional business leaders was a big issue for HR – one that, because of its difficulty, would have been easy to push off. Seeing the extent to which inaction could be holding back business performance created a greater sense of urgency.[296]

What do the C-level executives really want from HR that you can use as hooks to start and continue the transformation? Sojourne Partners (2020) brought together a group of CEOs and CFOs with HR to ask them this question. These were their 12 key observations:

---

296 Charan et al., 2015.

1. Show the numbers. Map everything you do back to the numbers.

2. Come prepared. Why is your proposal important? What is the strategic link and the ROI? What is the change impact? Are there other possible solutions?

3. Know the business of your business. Spend meaningful time across the entire value chain of the organisation to understand enablers and barriers and build strong relationships.

4. Start small by grabbing the low hanging fruit. Get some small wins to gain credibility and demonstrate new ideas.

5. Own that you are a mentor and coach. Share your perspective on all matters as an equal at the table. Challenge appropriately.

6. Start dialogues. Bring people into critical conversations early and often.

7. Approach each individual C-suite member uniquely to get the most out of them.

8. Your brand is important. Market your function and its achievements.

9. Find other advocates. Find allies and advocates in the C-suite team who understand what you want to achieve and partner with you.

10. Ask and ask again. Never give up if you believe something is important.

11. Build relationships. Take time to understand people and their challenges.

12. Communicate. Let people know how you and your team are progressing on issues, what your assumptions and reasonings are behind decisions and initiatives, and support C-suite executives in their organisational messaging.

You have to report your key outcomes and tell powerful stories

Leading companies such as Google, Best Buy, P&G and Sysco use sophisticated data- collection technology and analysis to get the most value from their talent. Solid proof regarding the business impact of human resource management gets the attention of business executives, however identifying what to measure takes considerable effort. The chosen metrics must have a clear link to the value created for the business and employees to be meaningful. This means a new collaboration between HR and Finance to integrate and align metrics and get a more rounded view of how well business needs are being served. Most CEOs agree that they want commerciality, simplicity, talent and capability from HR. These are the areas that should be focused on and measured.

An HR leader who uses analytics properly to show business value will:

- calculate return-on-investment for (nearly) everything that they do;

- give evidence-based advice on how to drive the business from a people perspective;

- be pursued by line-of-business leaders to help them reach business targets;

- take accountability for a portion of the organisation's financial health;

- show results and not just HR activity completion (e.g. survey response rates); and

- create an HR strategy that has a direct impact on the bottom line.[297]

Deloitte[298] wrote that organisations should develop a comprehensive HR measurement and reporting strategy that is vertically aligned with the overall business strategy (leveraging the "top down" approach) and can provide varying levels of information as needed.

Organisations should develop a comprehensive HR measurement and reporting strategy that is vertically aligned with the overall business strategy (leveraging the "top down" approach) and can provide varying levels of information as needed.

HR Scorecards provide a snapshot of overall HR performance against strategic goals at a particular point in time, allowing executives and business leaders to monitor and manage the results of HR's key objectives. This strategically focused category of HR metrics and measures should be updated periodically, based on the timeline of an organisation's strategic goals. An example is shown in Figure 10.1.

---

297 Mondore et al., 2011.
298 Deloitte, 2016.

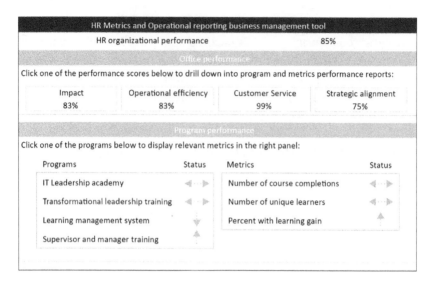

HR Metrics and Operational reporting business management tool		
HR organizational performance		85%

Office performance

Click one of the performance scores below to drill down into program and metrics performance reports:

Impact	Operational efficiency	Customer Service	Strategic alignment
83%	83%	99%	75%

Program performance

Click one of the programs below to display relevant metrics in the right panel:

Programs	Status	Metrics	Status
IT Leadership academy	◀ ▶	Number of course completions	◀ ▶
Transformational leadership training	◀ ▶	Number of unique learners	◀ ▶
Learning management system	▽	Percent with learning gain	▲
Supervisor and manager training	▲		

Figure 10.1: HR Scorecard examples[299]

HR Dashboards provide a more advanced way to assess metrics and Key Performance Indicators (KPIs), allowing organisations to present information in a more interactive and user-focused fashion. HR Dashboards are designed to be dynamic and visual, including charts and graphs that illustrate key trends and insights and enable stakeholders to filter information according to their needs. HR Dashboards help "manage the business" and are used to monitor and drive performance improvements across HR processes in support of broader leadership and organisational objectives, as shown in Figure 10.2.

299 Deloitte, 2016.

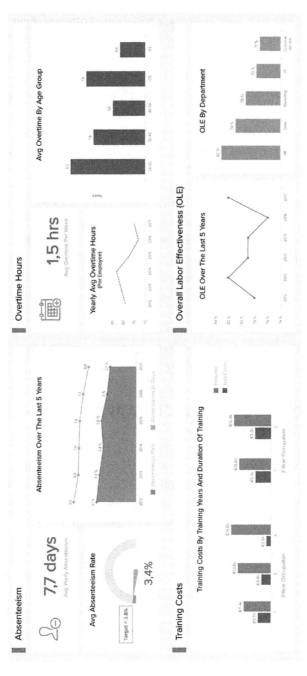

Figure 10.2: Klipfolio[300]

_____

300 Klipfolio, 2020.

In order to increase their awareness and value (both perceived and real), HR professionals need to learn how to sell their vision to the business. This means that when presenting the needs of your HR department to your business, you need to become a really good storyteller. HR's job is to craft their story (and the story of the business) into something meaningful that represents how you can help your business achieve the CEO's (and the overall business') vision more quickly. Allowing the CEO to understand what resources are required to achieve their strategy and vision is one of the most important things HR can do.

Narrative helps us to make sense of a world that is rapidly mutating, as compared to conventional management which is more suited to activities that are stable, linear and predictable. When you are able to illustrate, with clear examples, exactly how you can support your CEO's vision of the future, as well as how, in practical terms, you can make this happen, then half your battle is won. Start with a set of questions you want to show you have the answers for.

I end with the words of an inspiring Human Resource leader who is ensuring that she and her team stay relevant in disruptive times.

JESSICA DOURCY, CHIEF HAPPINESS OFFICER AT PALO IT

In her past life, Jessica Dourcy was a lawyer by training. She practiced employment law for a while before realising that the environment was much too rigid – or "static", as she called it – and decided to pursue other options. She fell into HR and hasn't looked back.

"I know what it means to be static and I don't believe that this worked", she said. "It worked in a certain context... but I have seen how this can feel for human beings when things don't move forward in the same time, in the same pace." To successfully adapt in an environment that's ever-evolving, she said that the only constant is change, so you have to be comfortable with it.

"HR can only help to promote success...[by] being keen on changing things on a regular basis", she said. "It makes me kind of excited to come to work and have things changing. It takes a bit of adjustment. At the beginning, I was like, 'I thought we've decided on that'." She added that about four years ago, prior to the organisation's transformation, if a strategy was decided and approved on by the board, it would have been left untouched for the rest of the year.

"HR is not static in this organisation", she said. "I miss the times when we decided on something in January and it's applicable across the year. It doesn't happen anymore in this industry. "If we decide on something, hopefully it will be relevant through the first quarter, but things change so fast – especially in a company like ours."

Now, policies and processes are always reviewed for the better, she explained. If the team feels that a policy they're deploying is not aligned with the ideal employee engagement, they're able to address the issues immediately. "Being in an agile company, it's very much in our DNA. Not having things changing means that we are losing relevancy, so I see this as a positive impact." Additionally, she shared that one of the greatest challenges and vital abilities for HR is to rise above "your ego" – or the way you're used to things being done.

"I think the biggest challenge is to learn to unlearn everything you know. That's extremely hard for us because we're all wired differently. If you speak to tech professionals, they would tell you that if they mastered a technology skill one day, it can become irrelevant the next day. We are all wired differently so we think we know something. We have a degree [in a subject] or whatever, and then we strongly believe that 'this is the way it should be'."

Dourcy's top advice for HR is simply "to be obsessed about forgetting everything you have learned" in terms of practices, so that you're able to keep relearning and remain relevant with the constant changes around you.[301]

---

301 Syed, 2019.

☑ Checklist

1. Are you making sense of the complex and changing world for your C-suite and Board?

2. Have you created a strong alliance with the CEO and CFO?

3. How have you shown up during COVID-19?

4. How are you leveraging this position?

5. How are you demonstrating impact and value?

6. What narratives are you using to position People and HR issues in the organisation?

LIST OF REFERENCES

Chapter 1

Accenture. (2016). *Liquid Workforce: Building the workforce for today's digital demands. Technology Vision.* Available from: https://www.accenture.com/fr-fr/_acnmedia/PDF-2/Accenture-Liquid-Workforce-Technology-Vision-2016-france.pdf

Aghina, W., De Smet, A. & Weerda, K. (2015). *Agility: It rhymes with stability.* McKinsey Quarterly. Available from: https://www.mckinsey.com/business-functions/organization/our-insights/agility-it-rhymes-with-stability

Bashinsky, A. (2020). *Focusing on tomorrow – Is HR planning for what the world will look like post Covid-19?* Available from: https://www.insidehr.com.au/is-hr-planning-for-what-the-world-will-look-like-post-covid-19/

Boland, B., De Smet, A., Palter, R. & Sanghvi, A. (2020). *Reimagining the office and work life after COVID-19.* McKinsey & Company. Available from: https://www.mckinsey.com/business-functions/organization/our-insights/reimagining-the-office-and-work-life-after-covid-19

Branson, R., Tomasdottir, H., Branson, H., Oelwang, J. & Gowridge, A. (2020*). Reimagining paths to employment. 100% Humans At Work.* London: The Virgin Foundation.

Deloitte. (2017). *Navigating the future of work.* Deloitte Review, 21. Available from: https://www2.deloitte.com/content/dam/insights/us/collections/issue-21/Deloitte-Review-Issue21.pdf

Dewhurst, M., Hancock, B. & Ellsworth, D. (2013). *Redesigning Knowledge Work.* Boston, MA: Harvard Business Review.

EY. (2018). *Why business must harness the power of purpose.* Available from: https://www.ey.com/en_za/purpose/why-business-must-harness-the-power-of-purpose

Hagel, J., Schwartz, J. & Wooll, M. (2019). Redefining Work for New Value: The Next Opportunity. *MITSloan Management Review.* Available from: https://sloanreview.mit.edu/article/redefining-work-for-new-value-the-next-opportunity/

Heerwagen, J. (2016). *The Changing Nature of Organization, Work and Workplace.* Available from: https://www.wbdg.org/resources/changing-nature-organizations-work-and-workplace

KPMG. (2019). *Future of HR 2020: Which path are you taking.* A Whitepaper by KPMG International. Available from: https://home.kpmg/xx/en/home/insights/2019/11/the-future-of-human-resources-2020.html

McGowan, H. & Shipley, C. (2020). *The Adaptation Advantage.* New York: John Wiley & Sons Inc.

McKinsey Global Institute Report. (2018). *Skill shift: Automation and the future of workforce.* Available from: https://www.mckinsey.com/featured-insights/future-of-work/skill-shift-automation-and-the-future-of-the-workforce

Mehendale, R. & Radin, J. (2020). *Welcome to the virtual age: Industrial 5.0 is changing the future of work.*Available from: https://www2.deloitte.com/us/en/blog/health-care-blog/2020/welcome-to-the-virtual-age.html

Mercer. (2020). *Designing for remote employee experiences.* Available from: https://www.mercer.com/our-thinking/career/designing-for-remote-employee-experiences.html

Novartis. (2020a). *Novartis Overview.* Available from: https://www.glassdoor.com.au/Overview/Working-at-Novartis-EI_IE6667.11,19.htm

Novartis. (2020b). *Novartis COVID-19 Response Fund provides support to healthcare workers and communities.* Available from: https://www.novartis.com/news/novartis-covid-19-response-fund-provides-support-healthcare-workers-and-communities

Shaninger, B., Zhang, H. & Zhu, C. (2020). *Demonstrating corporate purpose in the times of the coronavirus.* McKinsey Quarterly. Available from: https://www.mckinsey.com/business-functions/organization/our-insights/demonstrating-corporate-purpose-in-the-time-of-coronavirus

Sharifi, H. & Zhang, Z. (2000). A methodology for achieving agility in manufacturing organisations. *International Journal of Operations & Production Management. 20*(4), 496 – 513.

Swinburne University of Technology. (2019). *Peak Human Potential: Preparing workers for the digital economy.* National Survey Report. Centre for the New Workforce. Available from: https://www.swinburne.edu.au/news/2019/06/peak-human-potential-preparing-workers-for-the-digital-economy/

Ten Bulte, A. (2018). *What is Industry 4.0 and what are its implications on HRM Practices?* University of Twente. Research paper delivered at 11th BA Bachelor Thesis Conference. Enschede, The Netherlands.

Unilever. (2020). *Unilever Case study.* Available from: https://www.unilever.com.

World Economic Forum. (2019). *HR 4.0. Shaping People Strategies in the Fourth Industrial Revolution.* Available from: http://www3.weforum.org/docs/WEF_NES_Whitepaper_HR4.0.pdf

Chapter 2

Adidas Annual Report. (2019). *2019 Adidas Annual Report.* Available from: https://report.adidas-group.com/2019/en/

Deloitte. (2020b). *Combating COVID-19 with resilience.* Available from: www.deloitte.com/COVID-19

Deloitte. (2020). *The social enterprise at work: Paradox as a path forward.* 2020 Deloitte Global Human Capital Trends. Available from: https://www2.deloitte.com/content/dam/Deloitte/at/Documents/human-capital/at-hc-trends-2020.pdf

Green, K. (2019). *Why a Competitive People strategy is now critical?* Available from: https://www.linkedin.com/pulse/why-competive-people-strategy-now-critical-kevin-green/

Ind, N. (2019). *How Adidas Aligned Its People Strategy with Its Business Strategy.* Available from: https://strategicleaders.com/adidas-aligned-people-strategy/

KPMG (2018). Imagineering the future of the HR Organisation. Available from: https://home.kpmg/in/en/home/insights/2018/09/journey-futureready-hr-organization.html

Mercer. (2020). *The future of work: How to develop a People Strategy.* Available from: https://www.uk.mercer.com/our-thinking/thrive-series/how-to-develop-people-strategy.html

Nair, L. (2019). *HR 4.0. Shaping People Strategies in the Fourth Industrial Revolution.* Available from: http://www3.weforum.org/docs/WEF_NES_Whitepaper_HR4.0.pdf

Novartis. (2019). *Unleash the power of our people.* Available from: https://www.annualreview.novartis.com/at-a-glance/what-we-do/strategic-priorities/unleash-the-power-of-our-people.html

Strack, R., Bailry, A., Lovich, D., Baier, J., Messenbock, R., Ruan, F., Dyrchs, S. & Kotsis, A. (2020). *People Priorities for the New Now.* Available from: https://www.bcg.com/publications/2020/seven-people-priorities-in-reponse-to-covid

The Boston Consulting Group (BCG). (2006). *Opportunities for Action: When People Strategy Drives Business Strategy.* Available from: https://mkt-bcg-com-public-images.s3.amazonaws.com/public-pdfs/legacy-documents/file14856.pdf

Volkswagen. (2017). *Annual Report 2017: Shaping the Transformation Together.* Available from: https://annualreport2017.volkswagenag.com/group-management-report/sustainable-value-enhancement/employees.html

World Economic Forum. (2019). *HR 4.0. Shaping People Strategies in the Fourth Industrial Revolution.* Available from: http://www3.weforum.org/docs/WEF_NES_Whitepaper_HR4.0.pdf

Chapter 3

Accenture Consulting. (2017). *The New HR: Connected, Digital, Engaged.* Available from: https://www.accenture.com/bd-en/_acnmedia/pdf-52/accenture-new-hr-connected-digital-engaged.pdf

Bafaro, F., Ellsworth, D. & Ghandi, N. (2017). *The CEO's guide to competing through HR.* McKinsey Quarterly. Available from: https://www.mckinsey.com/business-functions/organization/our-insights/the-ceos-guide-to-competing-through-hr

BBVA. (2020). *Corporate Information.* Available from: https://www.bbva.com/en/corporate-information/#bbva-in-the-world

Capgemini Consulting. (2018). *Now or never – HR's need to shape its own future.* Available from: https://www.capgemini.com/consulting-de/wp-content/uploads/sites/32/2018/05/now-or-never-hrs-need-to-shape-capgemini-consulting.pdf

Cognizant. (2020). *An evolving profession: 21 New HR Jobs to Watch For.* Available from: https://www.cognizant.com/perspectives/an-evolving-profession-21-new-hr-jobs-to-watch-for

Deloitte. (2013). *Global Business Driven HR Transformation: The Journey Continues.* Available from: https://www2.deloitte.com/content/dam/Deloitte/de/ Documents/human-capital/global-business-driven-hr-transformation.pdf

Deloitte. (2018). *Global Human Capital Trends: The Rise of the social enterprise.* Available from: https://www2.deloitte.com/content/dam/insights/us/articles/ HCTrends2018/2018-HCtrends_Rise-of-the-social-enterprise.pdf

Deloitte. (2020). *The social enterprise at work: Paradox as a path forward.* Available from: https://www2.deloitte.com/us/en/insights/focus/human-capital-trends/2020/technology-and-the-social-enterprise.html

Deloitte. (2014). *The High-Impact HR Operating Model: HR has a new mission. Here is the plan.* Available from: https://www2.deloitte.com/ie/en/pages/human-capital/articles/high-impact-hr-operating-model1.html

KennedyFitch. (2019). *From HR transformation to HR disruption to HR reinvented.* Available from: https://www.kennedyfitch.com/from-hr-transformation-to-hr-disruption-to-hr-reinvented/

KPMG. (2018*). Imagineering the future of the HR Organisation.* Available from: https://home.kpmg/in/en/home/insights/2018/09/journey-futureready-hr-organization.html

KPMG. (2019). *The future of HR 2019: In the Know or in the No: The gulf between action and inertia.* Available from: https://home.kpmg/xx/en/home/ insights/2018/11/the-future-of-human-resources.html

Lee, E. & Yu, K.S. (2013). *How are Global HR Competency Models Evolving for the Future?* Cornell University ILR School. Available from: http://digitalcommons. ilr.cornell.edu/student/17/

Mercer. (2020). *Designing for remote employee experiences.* Available from: https:// www.mercer.com/our-thinking/career/designing-for-remote-employee-experiences.html

Orange. (2016). *What role for HR in 2020-2025?* Available from: https://www. oliverwyman.com/content/dam/oliver-wyman/global/en/2016/june/ What%20role%20for%20HR%20in%202020-2025.pdf

Schotkamp, T. & Danoesastro, M. (2018). *HR's pioneering role in Agile at ING.* Available from: https://www.bcg.com/en-za/publications/2018/human-resources-pioneering-role-agile-ing

Ulrich, D. (1996). *Human Resource Champions: The Next Agenda for Adding Value and Delivering Results.* Boston: Harvard Business Review Press.

World Economic Forum. (2019). *HR 4.0. Shaping People Strategies in the Fourth Industrial Revolution.* Available from: http://www3.weforum.org/docs/WEF_ NES_Whitepaper_HR4.0.pdf

Zeolli, M.L., Billeter, K., Stelle, S., Ferron, D., Fucello, J. & Garayzar, B.S. (2017). *The EY business-led people operating model.* Available from: http://docplayer. net/93100670-The-ey-business-led-people-operating-model.html

Chapter 4

Acumen Academy. (2020). *Introduction to human-centered design*. Available from: https://www.acumenacademy.org/course/design-kit-human-centered-design

BasuMallick, C. (2019). *What is an Employee Persona?* HR Technologist. Available from: https://www.hrtechnologist.com/articles/employee-engagement/what-is-an-employee-persona/

BenefitExpress. (2019). *2016 Annual Enrolment Survival Guide*. Available from: https://www.slideshare.net/benefit_express/2016-annual-enrollment-survival-guide

Bersin, J. (2020). *Employee Experience. It's the #1 Issue at work – even right* now. Available from: https://www.linkedin.com/pulse/employee-experience-its-1-issue-work-even-right-now-josh-bersin/

Deloitte. (2019b). *Leading the social enterprise: Reinvent with a human focus*. Available from: https://www2.deloitte.com/content/dam/insights/us/articles/5136_HC-Trends-2019/DI_HC-Trends-2019.pdf

Deloitte. (2017). *Employee Engagement and Redefining the Employee Customer Experience*. Available from: https://www.slideshare.net/scoopnewsgroup/employee-engagement-and-redefining-the-employee-customer-experience

Deloitte. (2019). *The digital workforce experience: Getting technology to work at work*. Deloitte Review, Issue 25. Available from: https://www2.deloitte.com/content/dam/insights/us/articles/ca22677_the-digital-workforce-experience/DI_DR25-Digital-workforce-experience.pdf

Emmett, J., Schrimper, M., Wood, A. & Schrah, G. (2020). *COVID-19 and the employee experience: How leaders can seize the moment*. McKinsey Quarterly. Available from: https://www.mckinsey.com/business-functions/organization/our-insights/covid-19-and-the-employee-experience-how-leaders-can-seize-the-moment

Gartner. (2020). *Employee experience: Enhance your employee experience strategy to drive effective outcomes for both your employees and your organization*. Available from: https://www.gartner.com/en/human-resources/trends/employee-experience

Höfer, T. (2017). *Storyboarding 2.0!* Available from: https://sprintstories.com/storyboarding-2-0-4e282b2da94d

IBM Institute for Business Value. (2016). *Designing employee experience: How a unifying approach can enhance engagement and productivity*. Available from: https://www.ibm.com/downloads/cas/ZEND5PM6

KPMG. (2019). *Future of HR 2020: Which path are you taking?* Available from: https://home.kpmg/xx/en/home/insights/2019/11/the-future-of-human-resources-2020.html

KPMG. (2019). *The future of HR 2020: In the Know or in the No: The gulf between action and inertia*. Available from: https://home.kpmg/xx/en/home/insights/2018/11/the-future-of-human-resources.html

Lopushinsky, P. (2020). *Design Sprints for Employees: Creating A Better Employee Experience*. Available from: https://www.playficient.com/design-sprints-for-employees/

Managementkits.com. (2019). *The why, how, and what of employee experience design*. Available from: https://www.managementkits.com/blog/2019/4/8/the-why-how-and-what-of-employee-experience-design

Meister, J. (2016). *Cisco HR Breakathon: Reimagining the Employee Experience*. Available from: https://www.forbes.com/sites/jeannemeister/2016/03/10/the-cisco-hr-breakathon/#2e3a41a6f5ee

Mercer. (2020b). *Win with Empathy. Global Talent Trends Report*. Available from: https://www.mmc.com/content/dam/mmc-web/insights/publications/2020/may/Mercer-Global-Talent-Trends-2020-Executive-Summary.pdf

Mercer. (2020). *Designing for remote employee experiences*. Available from: https://www.mercer.com/our-thinking/career/designing-for-remote-employee-experiences.html

Netigate. (2020). *Measuring employee engagement efficiently and continuously*. Available from: https://www.netigate.net/whitepapers/measuring-employee-engagement-efficiently-and-continuously/

Oracle Human Capital Management. (2014). *An Employee Centric Approach to HR: Employee Experience Journey Mapping*. Available from: http://www.audentia-gestion.fr/oracle/employee-centric-hr-2203095.pdf

Ranosa, R. (2019). *These 100 companies have the happiest employees*. Available from: https://www.hcamag.com/us/specialization/employee-engagement/these-100-companies-have-the-happiest-employees/179556

Robertson, J. (2018). *What is digital employee experience (#DEX)? Step Two*. Available from: https://www.steptwo.com.au/papers/what-is-digital-employee-experience/

Roe, D. (2020). *How Remote Work Will Impact the Management of Employee Experience*. Available from: https://www.reworked.co/employee-experience/how-remote-work-will-impact-the-management-of-employee-experience/

Snowball, H. (2020). *We are moving from HR to HX: JLL's Helen Snowball*. Available from: https://www.peoplemattersglobal.com/article/employee-engagement/we-are-moving-from-hr-to-hx-jlls-helen-snowball-25415

Tucker, G. (2017). *Tucker & Company Employee Journey Map Example*. Available from: https://www.slideshare.net/GregTucker2/employee-journey-map-example

Willis Towers Watson. (2020). *Unilever embraces the digital revolution and enhances the employee experience*. https://www.willistowerswatson.com/en-AU/Insights/2020/05/hr-4-0-shaping-people-strategies-in-the-fourth-industrial-revolution

Yohn, D.L. (2016). *Design your Employee Experience as Thoughtfully as your Customer Experience*. Available from: https://hbr.org/2016/12/design-your-employee-experience-as-thoughtfully-as-you-design-your-customer-experience

Yohn, D.L. (2018). *Leaders and Losers in the Year of Employee Experience*. Available from: https://www.forbes.com/sites/deniselyohn/2018/12/26/leaders-losers-in-the-year-of-employee-experience/#1fa8b5d92381

Chapter 5

Ashoka & McKinsey & Company. (2018). *The skilling challenge: How to equip employees for the era of automation and digitization – and how models and mindsets of social entrepreneurs can guide us.* Available from: https://www. ashoka.org/sites/default/files/atoms/files/2018_the_skilling_challenge_ ashoka_mckinsey.pdf

Aurecon. (2018). *Australia's first visual employment contracts launched.* Available from: https://www.aurecongroup.com/about/latest-news/2018/may/visual-employment-contract#:~:text=05%20May%202018%20%E2%80%93%20 Global%20engineering,illustrations%20to%20complement%20the%20text.

Burrell, L. (2018). Co-creating the Employee Experience. *Harvard Business Review, 96*(2) p. 54.

Caglar, D. & Duarte, C. (2019). *10 Principles of workforce transformation.* Available from: https://www.strategy-business.com/article/10-principles-of-workforce-transformation?gko=d9b8b

Cappelli, P. & Tavis, A. (2018). HR goes agile. *Harvard Business Review, 96*(2) p. 46.

Cappelli, P. (2008). *Talent Management for the Twenty-First Century.* Available from: https://d1wqtxts1xzle7.cloudfront.net/32263933/Talent_Management_HBR-PDF-ENG.PDF?1383915054=&response-content-disposition=inline%3B+filename %3DTalent_Management_for_the_Twenty_First_C.pdf&Expires=1601996245&S ignature=OmGdVHpYeWAbN3DGXUy0wSdWgYoXV1D7nIBsmNumbdh2SABw7-K-8rxpOCY91-yFvmDvzwmSFxtzP37-n9QUYQIVSfW8ARt137Buz~Qy0y0CUiQ7-tXfgYAFS9TYKXtiT6Gw3xUliKkKrc-1YlPfNM5fyTzqArnQnCkxMb3OUUJhMxBBp vQtYjb3Mc-pN9Z6QWNAmei8ypCxA941evUjEFMoSv--r-iV6QE5Egjy6jEKp7GA-ZQ9Skh2-m7-Y6M3GhX22kNbJJh3vtWI7WeY8Qntu880xkjCJdRgaRCcDk bSHVDYWttrxWVUIeHeDK1kp0RE6U3LGgGYEGFvW1L~KA__&Key-Pair-Id=APKAJLOHF5GGSLRBV4ZA

Corzo, C. (2016). *Candidate Experience in a VUCA world.* ATC 2016.

Deloitte. (2014). *High-Impact Learning Organization Study.* Available from: https:// www2.deloitte.com/content/dam/insights/us/articles/hc-trends-2014-diversity-to-inclusion/GlobalHumanCapitalTrends_2014.pdf

Deloitte. (2017). *Future of Work. The People Imperative.* Available from: https:// pdf4pro.com/view/future-of-work-deloitte-5bb044.html

Deloitte. (2018). *Global Human Capital Trends: The Rise of the social enterprise.* Available from: https://www2.deloitte.com/content/dam/insights/us/articles/ HCTrends2018/2018-HCtrends_Rise-of-the-social-enterprise.pdf

Doig, C. (2019). *The X-shaped learner.* Available from: https://www.thinkbeyond. co.nz/blog/x-shaped-learner/.

Donovan, J. & Benko, C. (2016) AT&T's Talent Overhaul. *Harvard Business Review.* 68-73. Available from: https://hbr.org/2016/10/atts-talent-overhaul

EFMD Global. (2018). *Digital Age Learning. EFMD Special Interest Group Report.* Available from: https://www.efmdglobal.org/wp-content/uploads/5a_SIG_ DAL_Report.pdf

Ewenstein, B., Hancock, B. & Komm, A. (2016). *Ahead of the curve. The future of performance management.* Available from: https://www.mckinsey.com/business-functions/organization/our-insights/ahead-of-the-curve-the-future-of-performance-management

Faethm. (2020). *About Faethm.* Available from: https://faethm.ai/about

Glaveski. (2019). *Where Companies go wrong with Learning & Development.* Harvard Business Review. Available from: https://hbr.org/2019/10/where-companies-go-wrong-with-learning-and-development

Haims, J., Stempel, J. & van der Vyver, B. (2015). *Learning and Development. Into the spotlight.* Deloitte Global Human Capital Trends report. Available from: https://www2.deloitte.com/us/en/insights/focus/human-capital-trends/2015/learning-and-development-human-capital-trends-2015.html

Hallenbeck,G., Horney, N. & Bateman, S. (2018). *Redefining Talent for the New World of Work.* Center for Creative Leadership. Available from: https://www.ccl.org/articles/white-papers/redefining-talent-with-talent-portfolio-agility/

Hancock, B., Lazaroff-Puck, K. & Rutherford, S. (2020). *Getting practical about the future of work.* McKinsey Quarterly. Available from: https://www.mckinsey.com/business-functions/organization/our-insights/getting-practical-about-the-future-of-work

Heidrick & Struggles. (2020). *Priming performance management.* Available from: https://www.heidrick.com/Knowledge-Center/Publication/Priming_performance_management

Johnson, D. (2014). *Getting from 70-20-10 to Continuous Learning.* Bersin by Deloitte. Available from: https://www2.deloitte.com/content/dam/Deloitte/at/Documents/human-capital/research-bulletin-2014.pdf

McGowan, H.E. (2019). *Learning is the New Pension.* Available from: https://www.forbes.com/sites/heathermcgowan/2019/10/29/learning-is-the-new-pension/#78dfc8b6661a

Mercer. (2015). *Talent Ecosystems: Manage Critical Capabilities to Gain a Competitive Edge.* Available from: https://www.mercer.com.au/content/dam/mercer/attachments/asia-pacific/australia/Talent/mercer-talent-ecosystems.pdf

Mercer. (2020b). *Win with Empathy. Global Talent Trends Report.* Available from: https://www.mmc.com/content/dam/mmc-web/insights/publications/2020/may/Mercer-Global-Talent-Trends-2020-Executive-Summary.pdf

Morris, D. (2016). *Death to the Performance Review: How Adobe Reinvented Performance Management and Transformed its Business.* World at Work Journal. Available from: https://www.adobe.com/content/dam/acom/en/aboutadobe/pdfs/death-to-the-performance-review.pdf

Murlidhar, N. (2020). *Leading with learning: putting L&D at the heart of your business strategy.* Available from: https://www.trainingzone.co.uk/deliver/training/leading-with-learning-putting-ld-at-the-heart-of-your-business-strategy#:~:text=Putting%20learning%20and%20development%20at,ensuring%20they're%20prepared%20as

Schouten, M. & Munshi, P. (2020). *Skills Expander: Tackling the challenges of upskilling and job transformation*. Available from: https://www.pwc.com/sg/en/publications/upskilling-for-competitiveness-and-employability.html

Van Dam, N. & Coates, K. (2020). *How to turn in-person leadership programs into highly effective virtual classroom programs*. IEPublishing. Available from: https://docs.ie.edu/center-for-corporate-learning-innovation/publications/How-to-turn-in-person-leadership-programs-into-highly-effective-virtual-classroom-programs.pdf

Van Dam, N. (2018). *Elevating Learning and Development: Insights and Practical Guidance from the Field*. New York: McKinsey & Company.

World Economic Forum (WEF). (2020). *Diversity, Equity and Inclusion 4.0: A toolkit for leaders to accelerate social progress in the future of work*. Available from: https://www.weforum.org/reports/diversity-equity-and-inclusion-4-0-a-toolkit-for-leaders-to-accelerate-social-progress-in-the-future-of-work

Chapter 6

Crozier. (2020). R. *NAB uses "people analytics" to unlock power of 40k staff*. Available from: https://humanengineers.com/nab-uses-people-analytics-to-unlock-power-of-40k-staff/

Deloitte. (2018). *Global Human Capital Trends: The Rise of the social enterprise*. Available from: https://www2.deloitte.com/content/dam/insights/us/articles/HCTrends2018/2018-HCtrends_Rise-of-the-social-enterprise.pdf

Deloitte. (2018). *Robotics and cognitive automation in HR*. Available from: https://www2.deloitte.com/content/dam/Deloitte/us/Documents/process-and-operations/us-cons-robotics-and-cognitive-automation-in-hr.pdf

EY. (2018). *The new age artificial intelligence for human resource opportunities and functions*. Available from: https://assets.ey.com/content/dam/ey-sites/ey-com/en_gl/topics/alliances/ey-the-new-age-artificial-intelligence-for-human-resources-010978-18gbl.pdf

French, M. (2019). *To Automate, Or Not to Automate, For HR, That Is the Question*. Available from: https://www.subscribe-hr.com.au/blog/to-automate-or-not-to-automate-for-hr-that-is-the-question#:~:text=The%20technological%20revolution%20has%20brought,be%20overwhelmingly%20positive%20or%20negative.

Green, D. & Gamel, G. (2018). *How to create career paths for People Analytics Professionals*. Available from: https://www.davidrgreen.com/blog/2018/7/26/how-to-create-career-paths-for-people-analytics-professionals

Green, D. (2020). Episode 17: *Using HR Analytics and Technology to drive business value at Unilever*. Available from: https://www.myhrfuture.com/digital-hr-leaders-podcast/2019/10/8/using-hr-analytics-and-technology-to-drive-business-value-at-unilever

Harbert, T. (2020). *People analytics, explained*. Available from: https://mitsloan.mit.edu/ideas-made-to-matter/people-analytics-explained

IBM Institute for Business Value. (2014). *Unlock the people equation: Using workforce analytics to drive business results*. Available from: https://www.ibm.com/downloads/cas/7JEENPAQ

Mercer. (2020b). *Win with Empathy. Global Talent Trends Report*. Available from: https://www.mmc.com/content/dam/mmc-web/insights/publications/2020/may/Mercer-Global-Talent-Trends-2020-Executive-Summary.pdf

Mondore, S., Douthitt, S. & Carson, M. (2011). Maximizing the Impact and Effectiveness of HR Analytics to Drive Business Outcomes. *People and Strategy, 34*(2), 20-27.

Nielsen, C. & McCullough, N. (2018). *How People Analytics can help you change process, culture and strategy*. Harvard Business Review. Available from: https://hbr.org/2018/05/how-people-analytics-can-help-you-change-process-culture-and-strategy

PWC. (2017). *How blockchain technology could impact HR and the world of work*. Available from: https://www.pwc.ch/en/insights/hr/how-blockchain-can-impact-hr-and-the-world-of-work.html

Randhawa, M. (2020). *How can HR become more data-driven and digital?* myHRfuture. Available from: https://www.myhrfuture.com/blog/2020/6/10/how-can-hr-become-more-data-driven-and-digital

Swift, M. (2018). *Using Big Data in HR for Industry 4.0 success*. Available from: https://focus.kornferry.com/future-of-work/using-big-data-and-analytics-in-hr-to-drive-success-in-the-fourth-industrial-revolution/

Van Vulpen, E. (2019). *15 HR Analytics Case Studies with Business Impact*. Available from: https://www.analyticsinhr.com/blog/hr-analytics-case-studies/

Visier. (2020). *How four companies enable their HRBPs with People Analytics*. Available from: https://www.visier.com/clarity/four-companies-enable-hrbps-with-people-analytics/

Chapter 7

Anthony, S., Gilbert, C. & Johnson, M. (2017). *Dual transformation: How to Reposition Today's Business While Creating the Future*. Boston, MA: Harvard Business Review Press.

Arena, M.J. & Uhl-Bien, M. (2016). Complexity Leadership Theory: Shifting from Human Capital to Social Capital. *People & Strategy, 39(2), p. 22-27.*

Bendell, T. (2014). *Building the anti-fragile organisation: Risk, Opportunity and Governance in a Turbulent World*. Aldershot, UK: Gower Publishing Ltd.

Berardino, J., McKenzie, M. & Harris, B. (2019). *True Transformation Demands That the CEO Act as the Chief Change Agent*. Available from: https://www.alvarezandmarsal.com/insights/true-transformation-demands-ceo-act-chief-change-agent.

Bushe, G.R. & Marshak. R.J. (2018). Planned and Generative Change in Organization Development. *OD Practitioner, 50*(4), 9-15.

Bushe, G.R. & Marshak, R.J. (2013). Advances in Dialogic OD. OD Practitioner. *Journal of the Organization Development Network, 45*(1), p. 1-4.

Bushe, G.R. (2019). Generative Leadership. *Canadian Journal of Physician Leadership, 5*(3), p. 141-147.

Carter, L. (2020). *Organizational Resilience: leadership lessons from COVID 19.* Available from: https://www.bestpracticeinstitute.org/blog/organizational-resilience-leadership-lessons-from-covid-19/

Carucci, R. (2014). *Microsoft's Chief People Officer: What I've Learned About Leading Culture Change.* Available from: https://www.forbes.com/sites/roncarucci/2019/10/14/microsofts-chief-people-officer-what-ive-learned-about-leading-culture-change/#2abc0781410d

CHO Group. (2015). *Accelerating transformational change: A CHO Group session with Gervase Bushe.* Available from: https://waldronhr.com/uploads/misc/acceleratingtransformationalchangewaldronlogo.pdf

Eoyang, G. & Holladay, R. (2013). *Adaptive Action: Leveraging Uncertainty in your Organization.* Available from: https://www.hsdinstitute.org/resources/leveraging-uncertainty-in-your-organization.html

Gallaghan, P.A. (2018). *GM's Internal Disruption Engine.* Available from: https://www.td.org/magazines/ctdo-magazine/gms-internal-disruption-engine

Innov8rs. (2018). *Necessary Disruption: The Path to Adaptive Spaces.* Available from: https://innov8rs.co/news/necessary-disruption-the-path-to-adaptive-spaces/

McKinsey. (2015). *The science of organizational transformations.* Available from: https://www.mckinsey.com/business-functions/organization/our-insights/the-science-of-organizational-transformations

Plexus Institute. (2018). *The Adaptive Space Imperative.* Available from: https://plexusinstitute.org/2018/06/11/the-adaptive-space-imperative/

Roper, J. (2018). *Defining OD: What is it and is HR doing enough?* Available from: https://www.hrmagazine.co.uk/article-details/defining-od-what-is-it-and-is-hr-doing-enough

Taleb, N. (2014). *Antifragile: Things That Gain from Disorder.* New York: Random House Trade.

The Boston Consulting Group (BCG). (2016). *Transformation: Delivering and Sustaining Breakthrough Performance.* Available from: https://media-publications.bcg.com/transformation-ebook/BCG-Transformation-Nov-2016.pdf

Chapter 8

Boston Consulting Group (BCG). (2020). *People Priorities for the New Now.* Available from: https://image-src.bcg.com/Images/BCG-People-Priorities-for-the-New-Now-Apr-2020_tcm9-245662.pdf

Beeson, J. (2014). *Five Questions Every Leader Should Ask About Organizational Design.* Available from: https://hbr.org/2014/01/five-questions-every-leader-should-ask-about-organizational-design

Deloitte. (2017). *The Organisation of the Future.* Global Human Capital Trends. Available from: https://www2.deloitte.com/us/en/insights/focus/human-capital-trends/2017/organization-of-the-future.html

Deloitte. (2018). *The Adaptable Organization: Harnessing a networked enterprise of human resilience.* Available from: https://www2.deloitte.com/content/dam/Deloitte/global/Documents/HumanCapital/adaptable-organization.pdf

Deshler, R. (2018). *Designing an Adaptive Organization.* Available from: https://alignorg.com/designing-an-adaptive-organization/

Galbraith, J. (2012). The Future of Organisation Design. *Journal of Organisation Design, 1*(1), p. 3-6.

LBL Strategies. (2020). *Mastering Agile Organizational Design For Public Sector Certification.* Available from: https://www.lblstrategies.com/training-and-certification/mastering-agile-organizational-design-for-public-sector-certification/

Kesler, G. & Kates, A. (2010). *Leading Organisation Design: How to Make Organisation Design Decisions to Drive the Results You Want.* San Francisco CA: Jossey-Bass.

Kimble. (2020). *Kimble tool.* Available from: https://www.kimbleapps.com

McKinsey. (2016). McKinsey on *Organization: Agility and Organization Design.* Available from: https://www.mckinsey.com/~/media/McKinsey/Business%20Functions/Organization/Our%20Insights/McKinsey%20on%20Organization/McKinsey%20on%20Organization%20Agility%20and%20organization%20design.ashx

Mercer. (2017). *Talent Trends 2017 Global Study: Empowerment in a Disrupted World.* Available from: https://www.benefitscanada.com/wp-content/uploads/2017/05/ca-2017-global-talent-trends-study-report-en.pdf

Mercer. (2020). *Win with Empathy. Global Talent Trends Report.* Available from: https://www.mmc.com/content/dam/mmc-web/insights/publications/2020/may/Mercer-Global-Talent-Trends-2020-Executive-Summary.pdf

Roux, M. (2019). *Project materials.* Roux Consulting Projects.

Reeves, M. & Deimler, M. (2011). *Adaptability: The New Competitive Advantage.* Available from: https://hbr.org/2011/07/adaptability-the-new-competitive-advantage

Salo, O. (2017). *How to create an agile organization.* Available from: https://www.mckinsey.com/business-functions/organization/our-insights/how-to-create-an-agile-organization

ServiceFutures. (2020). *What does it take to successfully design the organisation of the future?* Available from: https://www.servicefutures.com/what-does-it-take-to-design-the-organisation-of-the-future#:~:text=To%20design%20for%20the%20organisation,the%20plan%20to%20workplace%20actions.

Volini, E., Schwartz, J. & Roy, I. (2019). *Organizational performance: It is a team sport.* Available from: https://www2.deloitte.com/us/en/insights/focus/human-capital-trends/2019/team-based-organization.html

Chapter 9

Bariso, J. (2020). *Instead of Laying Off 20 percent of His Company, This CEO Made an Unusual Decision. It is a lesson in Emotional Intelligence.* Available from: https://www.inc.com/justin-bariso/instead-of-laying-off-20-of-his-company-this-ceo-made-an-unusual-decision-its-a-lesson-in-emotional-intelligence.html

CEC Report. (2017). *Leadership of the future: Skills and practices for better performance.* Accessed at https://www.cec-managers.org/wp-content/uploads/2017/07/CEC-Leadership-Report.pdf.

Clark, T.R. (2020). *The 4 Stages of Psychological Safety: Defining the Path to Inclusion and Innovation.* Oakland, CA: Berrett-Koehler Publishers.

De Smet, A. (2020). *Psychological safety, emotional intelligence, and leadership in a time of flux.* McKinsey Quarterly. Available from: https://www.mckinsey.com/featured-insights/leadership/psychological-safety-emotional-intelligence-and-leadership-in-a-time-of-flux

Delizonna, L. (2017). *High-Performing Teams Need Psychological Safety.* Available from: https://hbr.org/2017/08/high-performing-teams-need-psychological-safety-heres-how-to-create-it

Edmonson, A. (1999). Psychological Safety and Learning Behaviour in Work Teams. *Administrative Science Quarterly, 44*(2), p. 350-383.

Gloor, P.A. (2017). *Swarm Leadership and the Collective Mind: Using Collaborative Innovation Networks to Build a Better Business.* Bingley, UK: Emerald Publishing.

Haas, M. & Mortensen, M. (2016). *The Secrets of Great Teamwork.* Available from: https://hbr.org/2016/06/the-secrets-of-great-teamwork

Hawkins, P. (2018). *Tomorrow's Leadership and the Necessary Revolution in Today's Leadership Development.* Available from: https://www.talenttalks.net/wp-content/uploads/2017/05/GlobalResearchReport.BeExceptional.pdf

Kelly, R. (2019). *Constructing Leadership 4.0: Swarm leadership and the Fourth Industrial Revolution.* Kent, UK: Palgrave MacMillan.

Kim, L. (2017). *The Results of Google's Team Effectiveness Research will make you rethink how you build teams.* Available from: https://www.inc.com/larry-kim/the-results-of-googles-team-effectiveness-research-will-make-you-rethink-how-you-build-teams.html

Lectical. (2015). *LAP-1: Lectical Assessment in practice (LDMA Certification).* Available from: https://lecticalive.org/about/lap1#gsc.tab=0

Razzetti, G. (2020). *How to Use the Remote Culture Canvas.* Available from: https://liberationist.org/how-to-use-the-remote-culture-canvas/

Reams, R. (2020). *Maturing Leadership.* Bingley, UK: Emerald Publishing.

Redbooth. (2020). *Organized Work, Better Teams.* Available from: www.redbooth.com

Reynolds, R. (2020). *Why Purpose-Drive Leadership Matters Now More Than Ever: A Q&A with Pail Polman.* Available from: https://www.russellreynolds.com/insights/thought-leadership/why-purpose-driven-leadership-matters-now-more-than-ever-a-qa-with-paul-polman

Rock, D. & Grant, H. (2016) *Why Diverse Teams are Smarter*. Available from: https://hbr.org/2016/11/why-diverse-teams-are-smarter

Roux, M. (2020). *Leadership development in the future of work*. PHD research.

Singh, A. (2014). *Criticism of Trait Approach*. Leadership PSYCH 485 Blog. Available from: https://sites.psu.edu/leadership/2014/09/13/criticism-of-trait-approach.

Taylor, C. (2019). Why the CEO of this multi-billion-dollar firm wants to "unboss" companies - CNBC. Available from: https://future-business-ideas.blogspot.com/2019/10/why-ceo-of-this-multi-billion-dollar.html

Team Charter Canvas. (2020). *Play-In-Business.com*. Available from: *https://www.plays-in-business.com/download/team-charter-canvas-poster-a0-format/*

Van Dam, N. & Coates, K. (2020). *How to turn in-person leadership programs into highly effective virtual classroom programs*. IEPublishing. Available from: https://docs.ie.edu/center-for-corporate-learning-innovation/publications/How-to-turn-in-person-leadership-programs-into-highly-effective-virtual-classroom-programs.pdf

Veldsman, T.H. & Johnson, A.J. (2016). *Leadership. Perspectives from the Front Line*. Randburg: KR Publishing.

World Economic Forum. (2019). *HR 4.0. Shaping People Strategies in the Fourth Industrial Revolution*. Available from: http://www3.weforum.org/docs/WEF_NES_Whitepaper_HR4.0.pdf

Chapter 10

Charan, R., Barton, D. & Carey, D. (2015). *People before Strategy: A new role for the CHRO*. Harvard Business Review. Available from: https://hbr.org/2015/07/people-before-strategy-a-new-role-for-the-chro

Caminiti, S. (2020). *How the coronavirus has elevated the role of HR Chiefs in the C-suite*. Available from: https://www.cnbc.com/2020/04/22/the-coronavirus-is-elevating-the-role-of-hr-chiefs-in-the-c-suite.html

Deloitte. (2016). *Enabling business results with "HR Measures that Matter"*. Available from: https://www2.deloitte.com/content/dam/Deloitte/us/Documents/human-capital/us-hc-enabling-business-results-with-hr-measures-that-matter.pdf

Donaldson, C. (2013). *Wesfarmers: why HR leaders need to work with boards*. Available from: https://www.insidehr.com.au/why-hr-leaders-need-to-work-with-boards/

Fanning, K. (2020). *HR departments everywhere are dealing with the fourth industrial revolution*. Available from: https://www.onlinemarketplaces.com/articles/31334-hr-departments-everywhere-are-dealing-with-the-fourth-industrial-revolution#:~:text=A%20new%20study%20dedicated%20to,the%20fourth%20industrial%20revolution%20approaches.&text=According%20to%20the%20study%2C%20the,physical%2C%20digital%20and%20biological%20worlds.

Gately, K. (2015). *Position of influence: How HR impacts business performance.* Available from: https://www.insidehr.com.au/position-of-influence-how-to-strengthen-hrs-ability-to-impact-business-performance/

Huffington, A. (2020). *How CHROs have met the moment.* Harvard Business Review. Available from: https://hbr.org/2020/06/how-chros-have-met-the-moment

Klipfolio. (2020). *Example HR Dashboard.* Available from: https://www.klipfolio.com/

Lee, T. & Wilkie, D. (2018). *How HR can earn the CEO's trust.* SHRM. Available from: https://www.shrm.org/hr-today/news/hr-magazine/1118/pages/how-hr-can-earn-the-ceos-trust.aspx

Mondore, S., Douthitt, S. & Carson, M. (2011). Maximizing the Impact and Effectiveness of HR Analytics to Drive Business Outcomes. *People and Strategy, 34*(2), p. 20-27.

Sojourne Partners. (2020). *C-Level Executives that empower their Human Resource Teams.* Available from: http://www.sojournpartners.com/c-level-executives-empower-human-resource-teams/

Syed, N. (2019). *How can HR stay relevant in disruptive times?* Available from: https://www.hcamag.com/au/specialisation/leadership/how-can-hr-stay-relevant-in-disruptive-times/164031

INDEX

T

U

V

W

CPSIA information can be obtained
at www.ICGtesting.com
Printed in the USA
LVHW021816280423
745572LV00008B/322